MONTHLY MAGICKAL RECORD

BY KELLY CREE + JESSICA MULLEN

school of
life design

Published 2018 by Kelly Cree and Jessica Mullen.
This work is released to the public domain.

ISBN:
978-0-359-05983-6

TYPEFACES:
Adobe Caslon Pro
Mason Sans OT
Moon

WHAT IS SCHOOL OF LIFE DESIGN?

Founded in 2010 by graphic designers Kelly Cree and Jessica Mullen,
The School of Life Design (SoLD) aims to provide a formal education
in spirituality. Imagine if mindfulness, presence, and joy were taught in
schools. What if we were taught from a young age how to leverage our
innate magickal abilities instead of encouraged to suppress them?
Employing the principles of design—harmony, balance, hierarchy, scale,
focus, and contrast—SoLD pragmatically fills the spiritual void left by
public education. Offering conscious creation resources from positive
thinking worksheets to guided meditations to Monthly Manifestation
Manuals, SoLD has everything you need to deliberately create and
enjoy your reality on a daily basis.

LEARN MORE AT

www.schooloflifedesign.com

TABLE OF CONTENTS

MAGICK
is the
METHOD
of SCIENCE
and the
AIM *of*
RELIGION

ALEISTER CROWLEY

introduction

This book was born out of a desire to refresh and revise our popular title, the *Monthly Manifestation Manual*. With updated calendars, a brand new Daily Ritual spread, and 31 unique exercises, the *Monthly Magickal Record* combines the utility of a day planner with the witch-craft of a modern Book of Shadows.

The founder of modern magick, Aleister Crowley, believed in a scientific approach to mysticism, recommending recording spiritual progress in a diary. It is an effective method for mastering your magickal practice by helping you recognize repeatable regularities. This book will help you learn what magickal concepts work for you.

There is no prerequisite for the *Monthly Magickal Record*. If you have already experienced the *Monthly Manifestation Manual*, you will find this book takes what you learned from your *MMM* and pushes it further.

Inspired by Don Miguel Ruiz's *The Four Agreements*, we named each new exercise a "spell" to emphasize the power of words. Words are spells we cast on the world, and what we say and think completely influences reality as we know it. Every single utterance from your consciousness affects your experience, so we created this journal for harnessing, organizing and wielding that power.

Magick works best when you make it a daily practice, but there is no requirement to use this record every day. Sometimes, stepping away from spellwork is necessary for manifestation. When you forget you ever wanted it, you find it's already yours.

However, there is a Daily Ritual spread and companion exercise for each day of a 31-day month. Weaving this book into a deliberate daily practice reveals the dimension of magick and synchronicity, training your attention into the perfection of the present moment.

We made this book because we know the satisfaction of transmuting pain into love. Every negative aspect of your life can now bring you the pleasure of feeling better and all the manifestations that come with a good mood. Your mood is your work, because it is the way you feel that attracts your circumstances. Let the *Monthly Magickal Record* help you feel the best you've ever felt, and before long your reality will appear as heaven on earth!

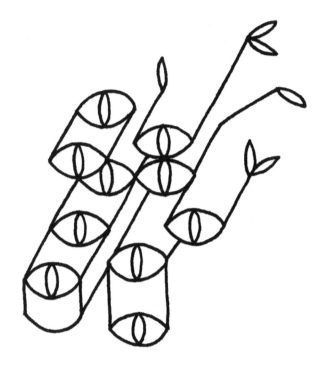

this is the magickal
record of

this month i intend

_____

_____

_____

MAGICKAL CALENDARS

Welcome to the time-based portion of this journal. Up first is a blank month-at-a-glance page for visualizing the next several weeks of your journey here on planet Earth. Pencil in the dates of your current month.

Beyond the month view lies six spreads of seven-day weeks. Use this section as you would a magickal day planner, noting your appointments and your gratitudes. When you appreciate what you have, you attract more.

Beside each date field are three spaces labeled "B," "L," and "D". This is for breakfast, lunch and dinner meal planning. We included these spaces because nutrition can have a big impact on magickal powers. Not having to wonder about what you're going to eat makes space for upper-level operations.

Discard your to-do list for a to-not-give-a-fuck about list, which asks you to imagine what it would feel like to truly let go of needing to check items off a list to feel good. When you do not give a fuck if you get something done, you will find the universe makes arrangements for you.

SUNDAY MONDAY TUESDAY WEDNESDAY THURSDAY FRIDAY SATURDAY

MONTH OF _____

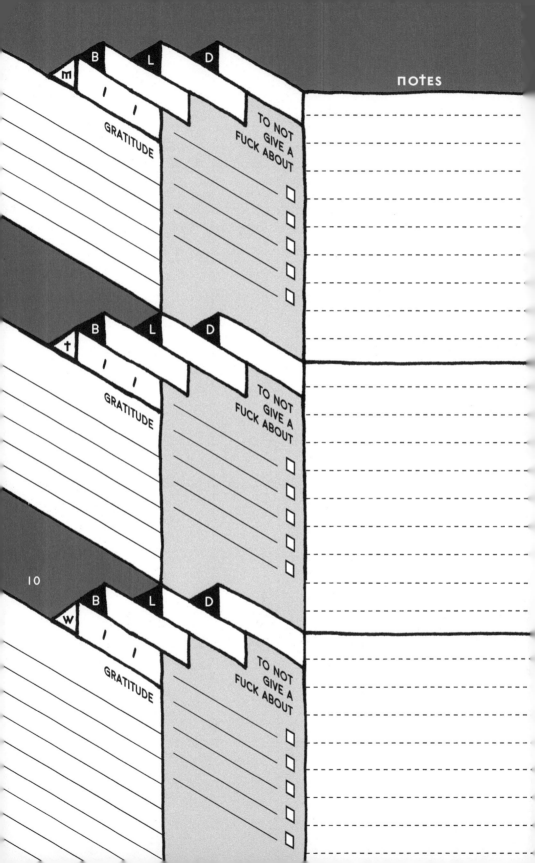

B L D

m

GRATITUDE

TO NOT
GIVE A
FUCK ABOUT

☐
☐
☐
☐
☐

B L D

†

GRATITUDE

TO NOT
GIVE A
FUCK ABOUT

☐
☐
☐
☐
☐

10

B L D

W

GRATITUDE

TO NOT
GIVE A
FUCK ABOUT

☐
☐
☐
☐
☐

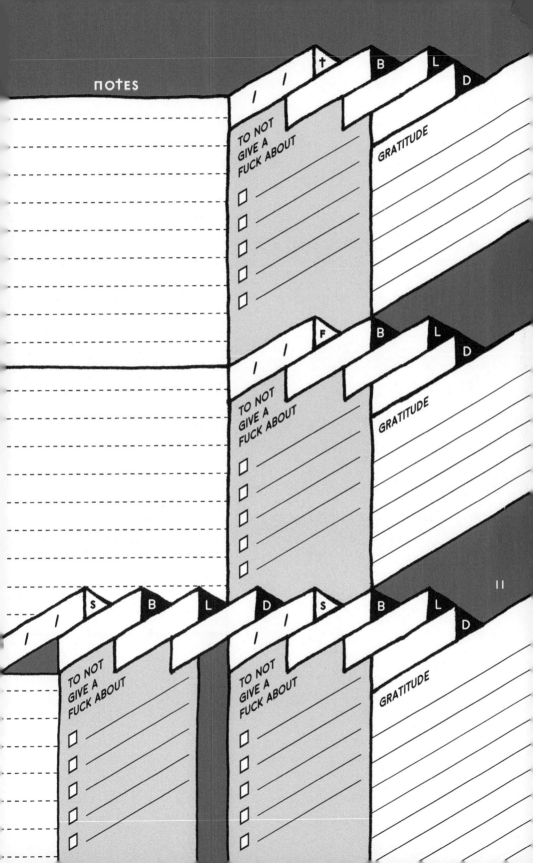

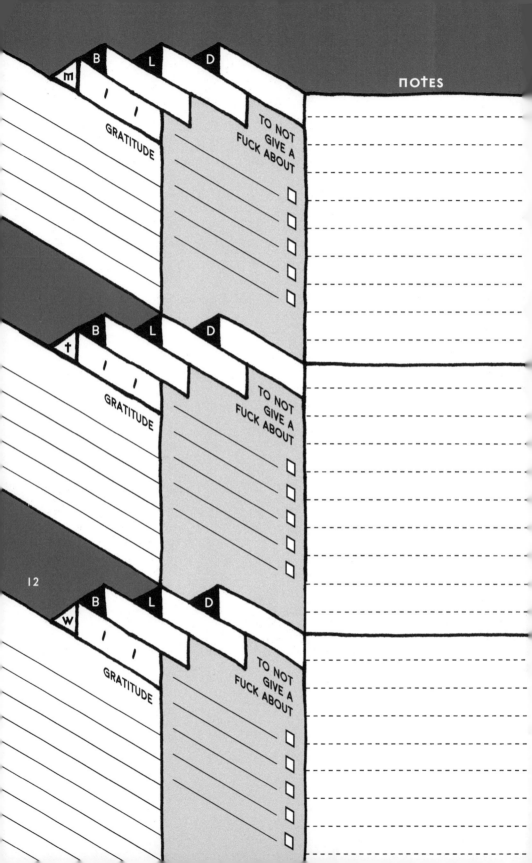

B L D

m

GRATITUDE

TO NOT
GIVE A
FUCK ABOUT

☐
☐
☐
☐
☐

B L D

†

GRATITUDE

TO NOT
GIVE A
FUCK ABOUT

☐
☐
☐
☐
☐

12

B L D

w

GRATITUDE

TO NOT
GIVE A
FUCK ABOUT

☐
☐
☐
☐
☐

TO NOT
GIVE A
FUCK ABOUT

☐ _____
☐ _____
☐ _____
☐ _____
☐ _____

/ / † B L D

GRATITUDE

TO NOT
GIVE A
FUCK ABOUT

☐ _____
☐ _____
☐ _____
☐ _____

/ / F B L D

GRATITUDE

/ / S B L D

TO NOT
GIVE A
FUCK ABOUT

☐ _____
☐ _____
☐ _____
☐ _____
☐ _____

/ / S B L D

TO NOT
GIVE A
FUCK ABOUT

☐ _____
☐ _____
☐ _____

GRATITUDE

B L D

m

/ /

GRATITUDE

TO NOT
GIVE A
FUCK ABOUT

B L D

†

/ /

GRATITUDE

TO NOT
GIVE A
FUCK ABOUT

14

B L D

w

/ /

GRATITUDE

TO NOT
GIVE A
FUCK ABOUT

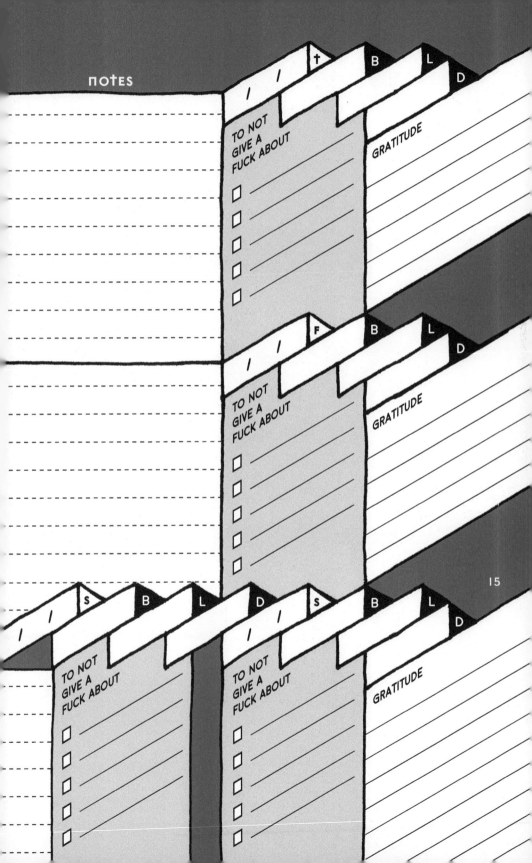

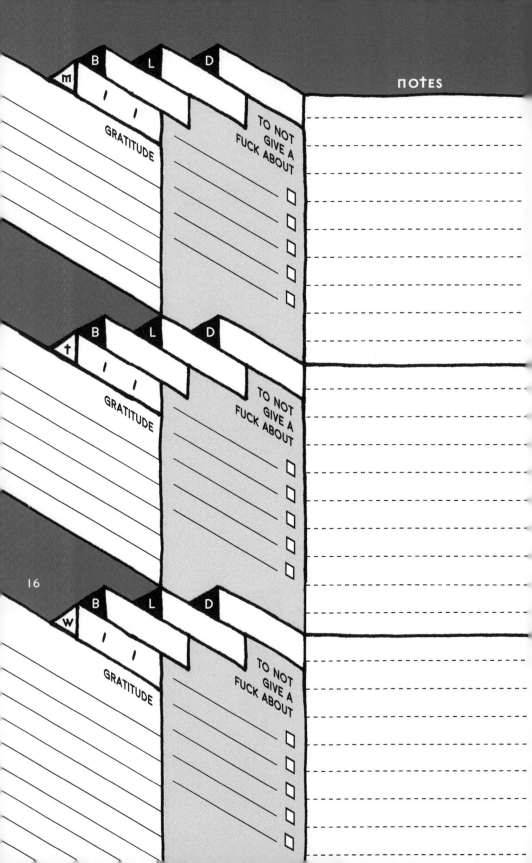

B L D

m

GRATITUDE

TO NOT
GIVE A
FUCK ABOUT

☐
☐
☐
☐
☐

B L D

†

GRATITUDE

TO NOT
GIVE A
FUCK ABOUT

☐
☐
☐
☐
☐

B L D

w

GRATITUDE

TO NOT
GIVE A
FUCK ABOUT

☐
☐
☐
☐
☐

TO NOT
GIVE A
FUCK ABOUT

☐ _____
☐ _____
☐ _____
☐ _____
☐ _____

GRATITUDE

† B L D

TO NOT
GIVE A
FUCK ABOUT

☐ _____
☐ _____
☐ _____
☐ _____
☐ _____

GRATITUDE

F B L D

17

S B L D

TO NOT
GIVE A
FUCK ABOUT

☐ _____
☐ _____
☐ _____
☐ _____
☐ _____

S B L D

TO NOT
GIVE A
FUCK ABOUT

☐ _____
☐ _____
☐ _____
☐ _____
☐ _____

GRATITUDE

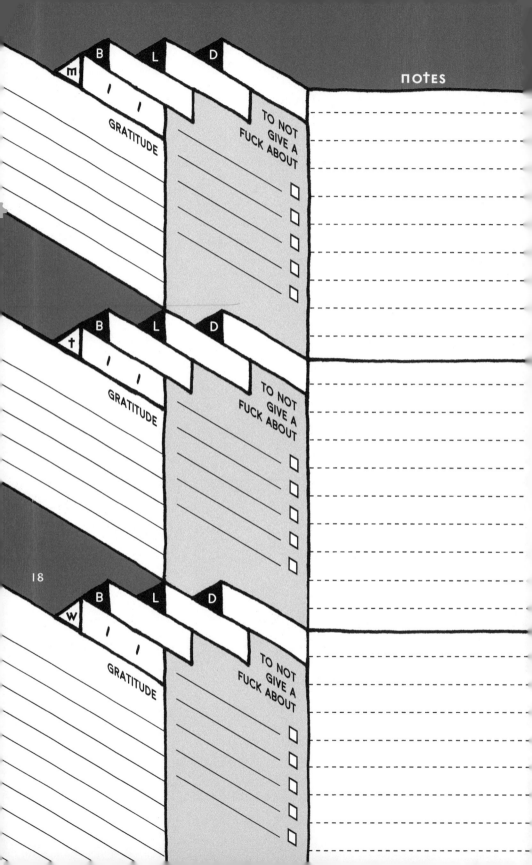

B L D

m

GRATITUDE

TO NOT
GIVE A
FUCK ABOUT

B L D

✝

GRATITUDE

TO NOT
GIVE A
FUCK ABOUT

B L D

w

GRATITUDE

TO NOT
GIVE A
FUCK ABOUT

TO NOT
GIVE A
FUCK ABOUT

GRATITUDE

TO NOT
GIVE A
FUCK ABOUT

GRATITUDE

19

TO NOT
GIVE A
FUCK ABOUT

TO NOT
GIVE A
FUCK ABOUT

GRATITUDE

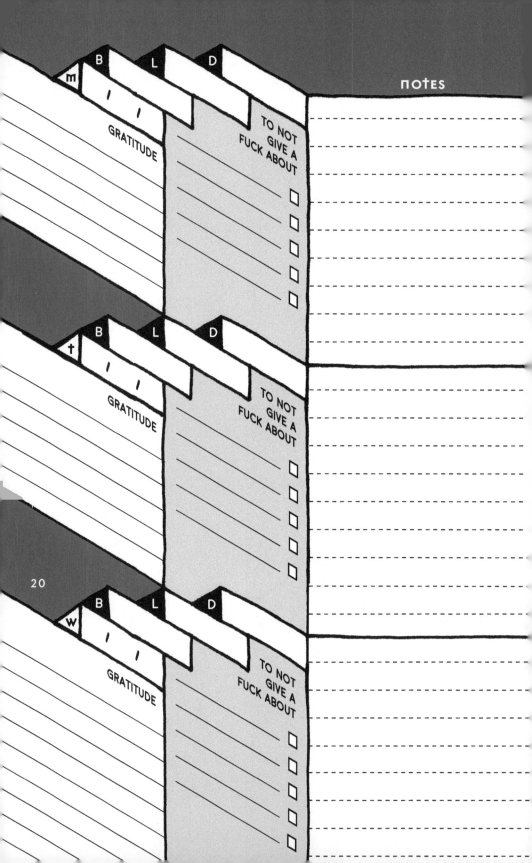

B L D

m

/ /

GRATITUDE

TO NOT
GIVE A
FUCK ABOUT

B L D

†

/ /

GRATITUDE

TO NOT
GIVE A
FUCK ABOUT

20

B L D

w

/ /

GRATITUDE

TO NOT
GIVE A
FUCK ABOUT

notes

/ / T B L D

TO NOT GIVE A FUCK ABOUT

- [ ]
- [ ]
- [ ]
- [ ]
- [ ]

GRATITUDE

/ / F B L D

TO NOT GIVE A FUCK ABOUT

- [ ]
- [ ]
- [ ]
- [ ]
- [ ]

GRATITUDE

/ / S B L D

TO NOT GIVE A FUCK ABOUT

- [ ]
- [ ]
- [ ]
- [ ]
- [ ]

/ / S B L D

TO NOT GIVE A FUCK ABOUT

- [ ]
- [ ]
- [ ]
- [ ]
- [ ]

GRATITUDE

DAiLY RiTUAL

The Daily Ritual includes divination, spell casting, pre-paving, intention setting, gratitude and visualization—everything you may need to practice conscious creation, mindfulness and manifestation. To begin, note the date, time and moon phase. This physical-world time tracking is useful for identifying patterns and synchronicities. There is also space to record a dream, whether it came to you in sleep last night or a daydream you can't stop imagining.

Next, ask your question. This could be about love, money, health, work, family, or something specific. Write your question and get to divining! The next three blocks provide space for recording the answers you receive in divination. Use your tarot decks, your runes, your pendulum, your tea leaves, or whatever else you may have at your disposal. Consult the oracles and note the answer.

Then we cast a spell! We borrow a prompt from Bashar, which helps us immediately begin living in our desired reality. "I am switching to the version of reality I prefer. In the reality I prefer…" and write your reality as you want it to be. Manifestation is just a shift in perception, and this spell casting can bring about immediate results.

Up next is pre-paving! This is a technique we learned from Abraham-Hicks, where you imagine a future event going exactly the way you want it to go, in order to mold your expectation and thus reality. First, name the event. Then write down the best that could happen before the event. What's the best that can happen during? And finally, how do you want to feel after the event?

Next, we set an intention, say a prayer, declare our love, and send forgiveness. These actions direct our energy, ask for help from the universe, tune ourselves to the highest vibration, and let go of our petty, ego-driven complaints.

Onto gratitude in advance! This powerful prompt asks you to say thank you for the things you want, as if you already have them. That is the core of manifestation—acting as if you already have the thing you want, and really feeling as good as if you did. Think about what you want, then start expressing your gratitude for it, as if you already had it. This gets you in the feeling place of having what you want, thus making you a magnet for it to come.

Then note how you want to feel. Everything we want to manifest, we want because we think it will make us feel better. What if we just chose to feel that good first? We wouldn't need the manifestation! So identify what it is that you really want to feel, and take a moment to practice what it would feel like to feel that way. You don't need anything outside of yourself to be happy, it can all be generated from within.

If meditation is something you do, there is space for insights and epiphanies. Otherwise the space can be used to make notes about your rituals and magick. Up to you!

Finally, consult your guides. This blank box is perfect for doodling and intuiting. Quiet your mind and listen for what advice you hear. You can try drawing with your non-dominant hand to see what your subconscious wants to tell you. Or draw a vision you've had, or a visualization of something you want. Let this be a space to uncover your inner wisdom, however it may come about.

31 UNIQUE SPELLS

Between each Daily Ritual spread is a different mind training activity. Two are for visualization, to open your imagination to your manifesting and healing powers. Eight involve mantra repetition, which trains new neural pathways in your brain, resulting in new patterns of thought. Five focus on gratitude and appreciation because what you notice, you get more of. Two exercises are for practicing channeling, which strengthens your connection to infinite intelligence. Five are about the concept of awareness, and how simply watching your thoughts brings about peace. Four explore the power of intention, and five practices ask you to transmute negative experiences into positive expectation.

These mental games are designed to help you find peace in your mind and joy in your heart. They remind you that life is not serious and that your power lies in your perspective. Together, these 31 unique exercises provide a framework for incorporating magick into your daily life. Many of the spells include journaling prompts for rating your mood before and after completing the activity, so you can objectively gauge the effectiveness of each method.

Each individual spell was inspired by a different thought leader. Explore their work deeper via the "Further Reading" portion of each spread.

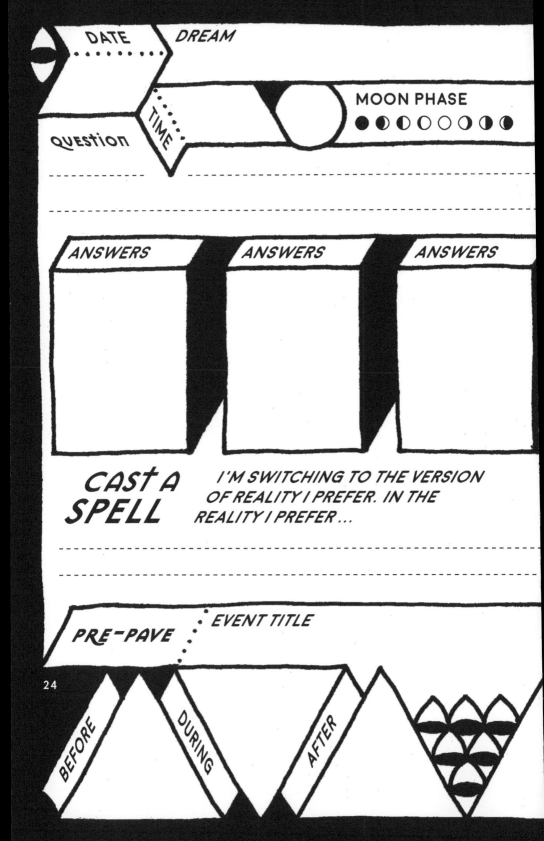

I INTEND

I PRAY

I LOVE

GRATITUDE
IN ADVANCE

I'M SO GRATEFUL

- - - - - - - - - - - - - - - - - - - -

I FORGIVE

- - - - - - - - - - - - - - - - - - - -

- - - - - - - - - - - - - - - - - - - -

- - - - - - - - - - - - - - - - - - - -

- - - - - - - - - - - - - - - - - - - -

I WANT
TO FEEL

- - - - - - - - - - - - - - - - - - - -

- - - - - - - - - - - - - - - - - - - -

- - - - - - - - - - - - - - - - - - - -

NOTES & EPIPHANIES

- - - - - - - - - - - - - - - - - - - -

- - - - - - - - - - - - - - - - - - - -

- - - - - - - - - - - - - - - - - - - -

- - - - - - - - - - - - - - - - - - - -

- - - - - - - - - - - - - - - - - - - -

- - - - - - - - - - - - - - - - - - - -

- - - - - - - - - - - - - - - - - - - -

- - - - - - - - - - - - - - - - - - - -

- - - - - - - - - - - - - - - - - - - -

VISIONS & GUIDES

SPELL FOR
vision

Everything you see physically manifested began as a vision. The most powerful technology, the truest love, the beach-iest vacation all were born in someone's imagination. The imagination is the birthplace of all manifestations.

Have you ever looked up and realized you have what you once wanted? It can be so easy to get distracted by always looking for the next manifestation that we forget to be conscious of all that we have already manifested for ourselves. In the midst of everyday life, it can also be difficult to remember to set aside time to think about what it is we *do* want instead of what we *don't*.

As you begin this journal, take some time to think about what you truly want. Give birth to it in your mind's eye. It's alive! Throughout the course of the next 30 days (or however you long you choose to use this Magickal Record), you will nurture and grow these newborn desires by nurturing yourself. As time goes on, if you start to wonder if your vision is manifesting into reality, don't. Know that it's already done. After you finish all of the exercises, return to this page and take note of all that was created in the background while you focused on harmonizing with the energy within.

instructions

For each category on this vision board, write, draw, or paste pictures of what you want. Be general if you have to, or be specific if you know exactly what you want. As you fill out this page, practice feeling what it would feel like to receive the things you want. There is no limit to what you can create in this life, so dream big! After you've completed the page, do your best to let the desires go and trust they're on the way.

FURTHER READING

ASK AND IT IS GIVEN BY ESTHER AND JERRY HICKS

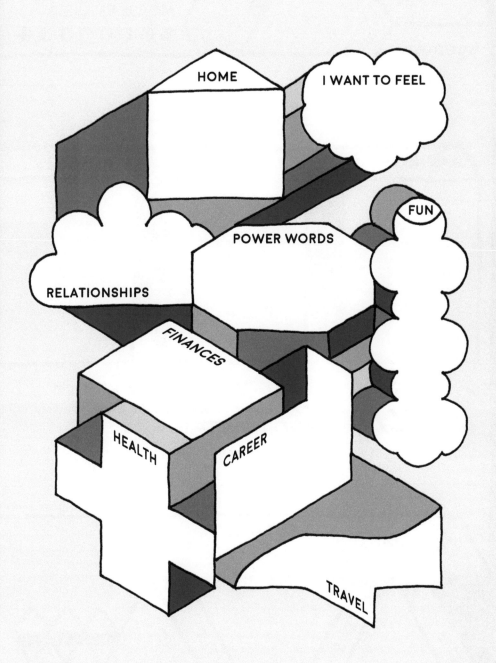

DATE

DREAM

MOON PHASE

●◐◑◑○○◑◑◐

QUESTION

TIME

- - - - - - - - - - - - - - - - - - - - - - - -

- - - - - - - - - - - - - - - - - - - - - - - -

ANSWERS

ANSWERS

ANSWERS

CAST A
SPELL

I'M SWITCHING TO THE VERSION
OF REALITY I PREFER. IN THE
REALITY I PREFER...

- -

- -

PRE-PAVE

EVENT TITLE

BEFORE

DURING

AFTER

I INTEND

I PRAY

I LOVE

GRATITUDE
IN ADVANCE

I'M SO GRATEFUL

I FORGIVE

I WANT
TO FEEL

NOTES & EPIPHANIES

VISIONS & GUIDES

CURING AILMENTS

> "The truth is to love yourself with the same intensity you would use to pull yourself up if you were hanging off a cliff with your fingers."
> KAMAL RAVIKANT

Do you love yourself? Do you intensely, authentically love yourself? Unfortunately, a lot of people do not. We spend a lot of time hating on ourselves in our minds–replaying sequences of times we've fucked up or imagining potential future transgressions. We might even think about how much we suck at life, how ugly or stupid we are, or what terrible people we are.

Just as the outside world mirrors the contents of our thoughts and emotions, so do our bodies. When you think, "I hate X about myself," or, "I'm a failure who will never amount to anything," those energies manifest physically in our bodies as ailments. When you think, "I love myself, I'm fabulous, and I deserve all the good that comes my way," that energy also manifests physically as well being. The two different thought patterns produce noticeably different physiological and emotional responses. Which one feels better?

Fill the space provided with the words "I love myself" and make an effort to feel that love with the same intensity you would use trying to save your own life in danger. Because that's what you're doing! When you say, "I love myself," you allow healing into your life. You allow well being into your body. You allow yourself to thrive, flourish and bloom.

On a scale of 1-10, rate your level of ease before and after completing this exercise. Do you feel more at ease?

BEFORE [ ]   AFTER [ ]

FURTHER READING

LOVE YOURSELF LIKE YOUR LIFE DEPENDS ON IT BY KAMAL RAVIKANT
YOU CAN HEAL YOUR LIFE BY LOUISE HAY

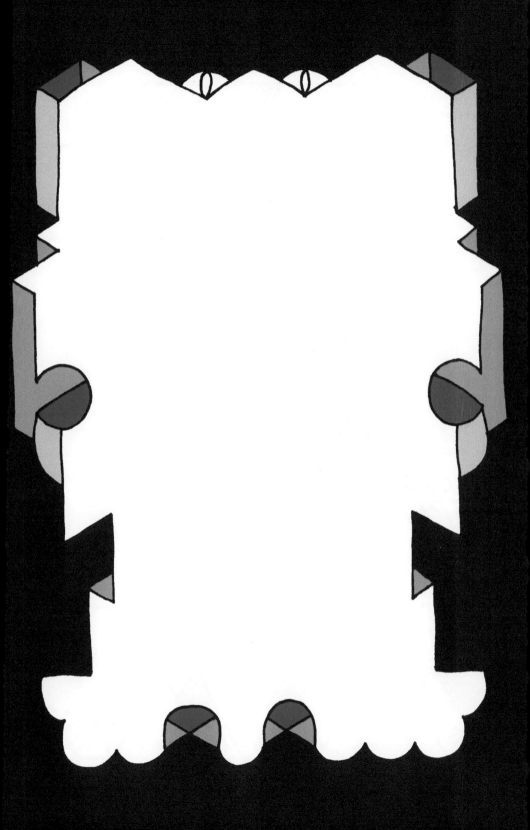

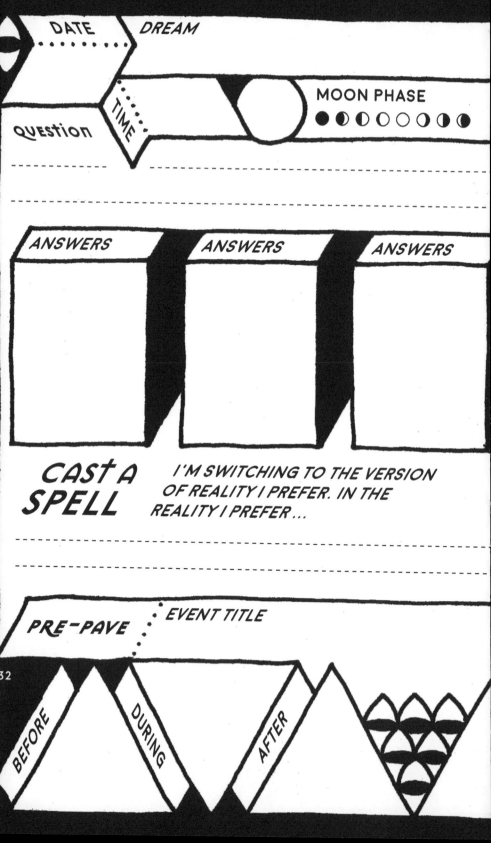

DATE

DREAM

QUESTION

TIME

MOON PHASE

ANSWERS

ANSWERS

ANSWERS

CAST A
SPELL

I'M SWITCHING TO THE VERSION
OF REALITY I PREFER. IN THE
REALITY I PREFER...

PRE-PAVE

EVENT TITLE

BEFORE

DURING

AFTER

I INTEND

I PRAY

I LOVE

GRATITUDE
IN ADVANCE

I'M SO GRATEFUL

I FORGIVE

I WANT
TO FEEL

NOTES & EPIPHANIES

VISIONS & GUIDES

SPELL FOR

BLESSINGS

Though his work was met with significant critical scrutiny in the scientific community for not being "science," Dr. Masaru Emoto presents an intriguing and compelling hypothesis. He claimed that vibrational energies could change the physical structure of water. Therefore, since the human body is mostly water, your vibration affects your body. Emoto claimed that water to which loving words were spoken produced beautiful crystals when frozen, whereas when hateful words were directed toward the water, its frozen form photographed as "ugly."

If you're using this workbook, you probably already have an inkling that not everything you experience can be proven empirically. Try convincing a scientist that chanting "Nam Myoho Renge Kyo" changed the entire dynamic of your relationship with your annoying neighbor and the scientist will scoff, chalking it up to coincidence. But you know your true power, even if nothing can "prove" it. So, let's test out Dr. Emoto's theory for ourselves and see if there's any proof in the ~~pudding~~ H_2O.

instructions
At the beginning of the day, imagine what you would look like if you were a frozen crystal. Base your interpretation on how you feel physically and emotionally. Draw what the crystal formation that is you looks like.

Throughout your day, remember to say only nice things to yourself. Important: Don't beat yourself up if you catch yourself thinking negative thoughts! Just notice the negative thoughts and let them go. At the end of the day, return to this exercise and interpret your vibration again in the form of a crystal. Is there any difference? Did the experiment work?

FURTHER READING

THE MIRACLE OF WATER BY DR. MASARU EMOTO

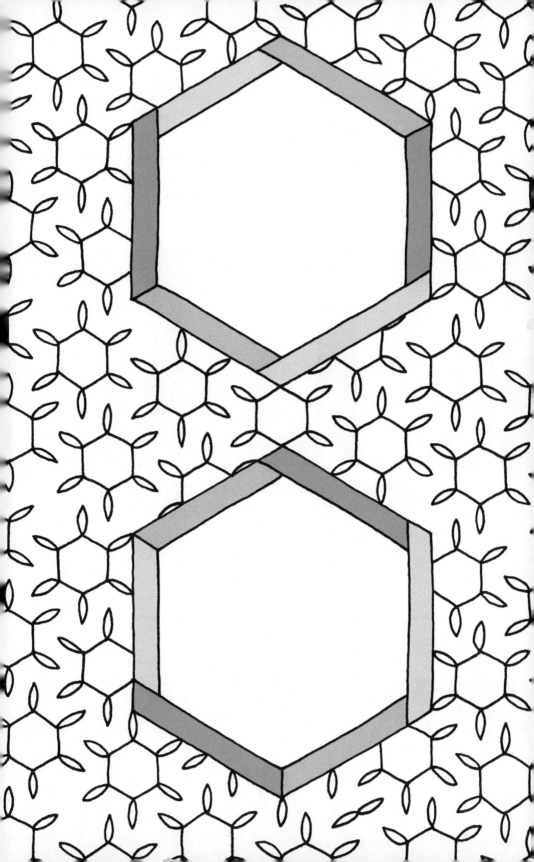

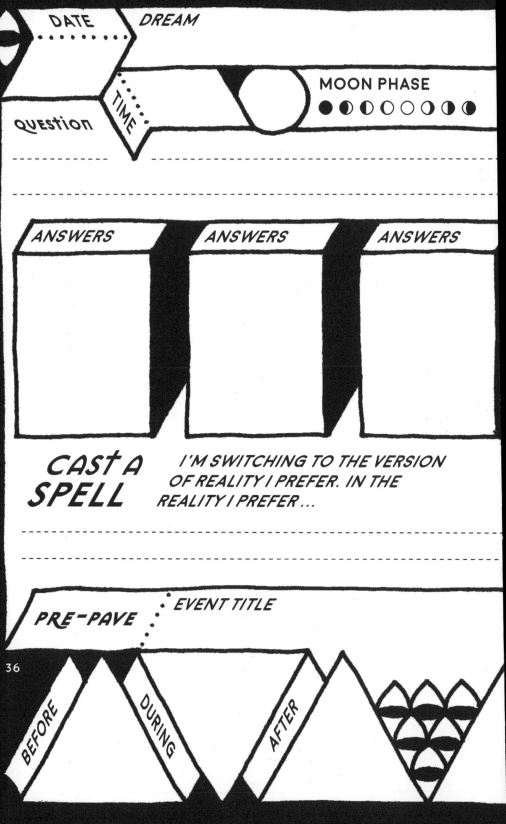

DATE

DREAM

MOON PHASE

QUESTION

TIME

ANSWERS

ANSWERS

ANSWERS

CAST A SPELL

I'M SWITCHING TO THE VERSION OF REALITY I PREFER. IN THE REALITY I PREFER...

PRE-PAVE

EVENT TITLE

36

BEFORE

DURING

AFTER

I INTEND

I PRAY

I LOVE

GRATITUDE
IN ADVANCE

I'M SO GRATEFUL

- - - - - - - - - - - - - - - - -
- - - - - - - - - - - - - - - - -
- - - - - - - - - - - - - - - - -
- - - - - - - - - - - - - - - - -
- - - - - - - - - - - - - - - - -
- - - - - - - - - - - - - - - - -

I FORGIVE

- - - - - - - - - - - - - - - - -
- - - - - - - - - - - - - - - - -
- - - - - - - - - - - - - - - - -
- - - - - - - - - - - - - - - - -

I WANT
TO FEEL

- - - - - - - - - - - - - - - - -

NOTES & EPIPHANIES

- - - - - - - - - - - - - - - - - - - -
- - - - - - - - - - - - - - - - - - - -
- - - - - - - - - - - - - - - - - - - -
- - - - - - - - - - - - - - - - - - - -
- - - - - - - - - - - - - - - - - - - -
- - - - - - - - - - - - - - - - - - - -
- - - - - - - - - - - - - - - - - - - -

VISIONS & GUIDES

SPELL FOR

WEALTH, PRODUCTIVITY AND SUCCESS

"Practice allowing your essential nature to shine by not enforcing judgements on yourself that were imposed by others. Remind yourself that you don't have to do anything: You don't have to be better than anyone else. Give yourself permission to just be. Lighten the burden you carry to be productive, wealthy and successful in the eyes of others."

DR. WAYNE DYER

How much of what you do on a daily basis is to please others? Do you find yourself constantly trying to succeed or achieve? Do you ever feel like you fill your entire day with doing and never get anything done? Or maybe it's not even for others, maybe you're constantly trying to be and do your best only for yourself. But why?

instructions

Take a break from striving today. In the spell candles provided, write lists of the things you think you need to do to be wealthy, successful and productive today, and then don't do a single one of them! Metaphorically allow the candles to burn, melting away your "to-do" list, one item at a time. This will probably be hard. You will feel useless. Worthless, even. But then you will feel free. Every time your mind tries to tell you that you absolutely must get that thing done, stop and allow yourself to exist for a moment without the expectation of achievement. Don't do anything you don't want to do!

Then, if any of the items call to you–if wild horses can't stop you from performing that task, then you'll know that is your true self carrying out that action, not the version of yourself that thinks you have to. If you simply MUST do something on this list after making the choice not to do any of it, you will know that you are doing that thing simply for the satisfaction of doing it, not because you think it will make you a better person. Then you will be your best self.

FURTHER READING

CHANGE YOUR THOUGHTS, CHANGE YOUR LIFE BY DR. WAYNE DYER

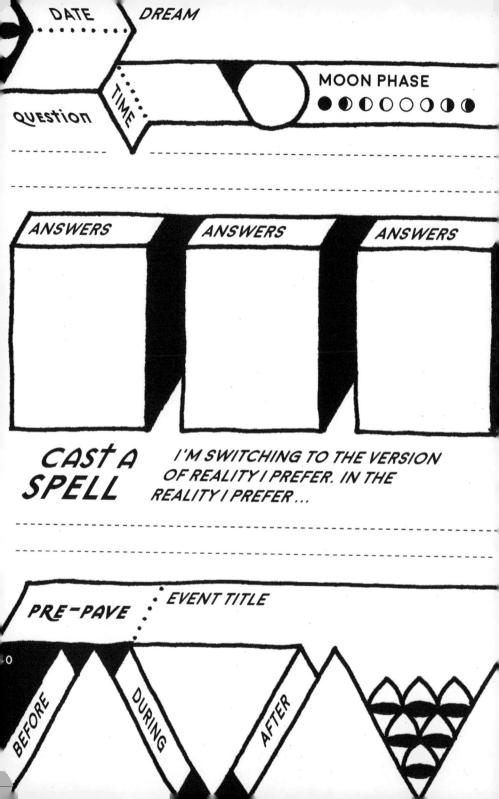

DATE   DREAM

QUESTION   TIME   MOON PHASE

ANSWERS   ANSWERS   ANSWERS

CAST A
SPELL   I'M SWITCHING TO THE VERSION
OF REALITY I PREFER. IN THE
REALITY I PREFER...

PRE-PAVE   EVENT TITLE

BEFORE   DURING   AFTER

I INTEND

I PRAY

I LOVE

GRATITUDE
IN ADVANCE

I'M SO GRATEFUL

I FORGIVE

I WANT
TO FEEL

NOTES & EPIPHANIES

VISIONS & GUIDES

SPELL FOR
ΜΑΠİFΕSΤİΠG

When you want something, it implies you don't have it. When you think to yourself, "I really want more income," you are affirming that you don't have enough income. You are creating a reality in which you don't have enough, perpetuating a lack mindset.

When you notice a desire, decide to choose it instead of want it. When you choose something, your thoughts align with having it. You can try thinking things like, "I am choosing more income," or, "I am so grateful for the money I make. I always have plenty." Your thoughts about the things you desire are creating your reality as you think them, so begin to choose the thoughts you want to be true.

After you switch from wanting to choosing, let the desire go and never think of it again. Your thoughts are constantly creating, and if you start wondering if your "choosing" worked, you're undoing the spell. You must stand firm in your knowing of your creative power. You no longer have to want the power to manifest what you want. You can choose to step into your power right now.

instructions

1. What do you want? Fill in the lines provided.

2. How does it feel to want it and not have it?

3. Choose instead of want. Finish the sentence, "I choose..."

4. How do you feel now that you've chosen it, instead of wanting it?

FURΤHER READİΠG

CONVERSATIONS WITH GOD BY NEALE DONALD WALSH

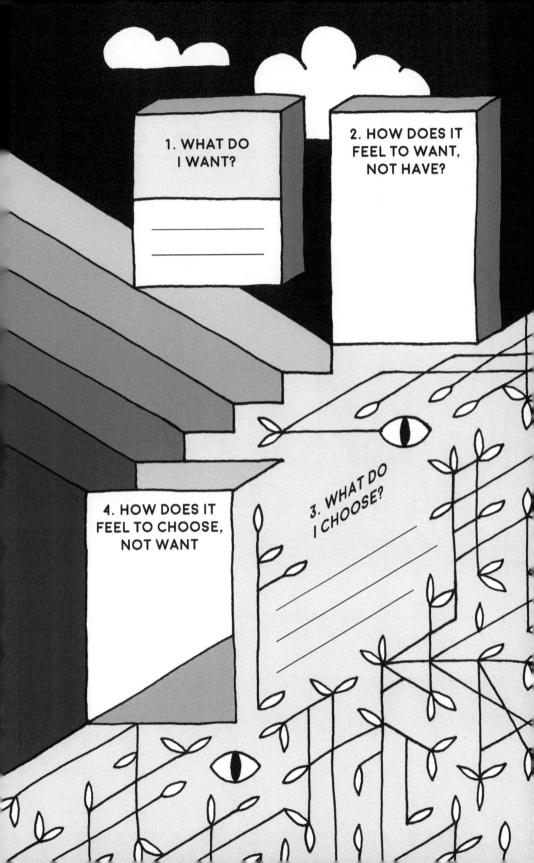

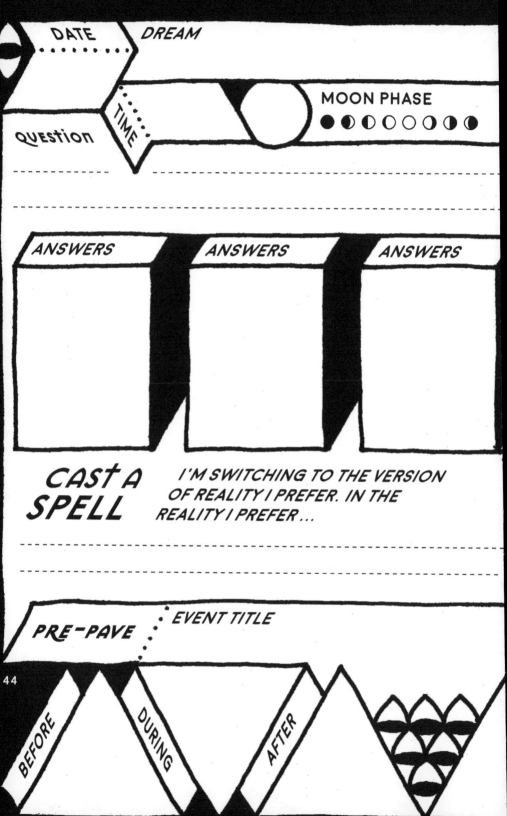

DATE   DREAM

QUESTION   TIME

MOON PHASE

ANSWERS   ANSWERS   ANSWERS

CAST A
SPELL

I'M SWITCHING TO THE VERSION
OF REALITY I PREFER. IN THE
REALITY I PREFER...

PRE-PAVE   EVENT TITLE

BEFORE   DURING   AFTER

I INTEND

I PRAY

I LOVE

GRATITUDE
IN ADVANCE

I'M SO GRATEFUL

- - - - - - - - - - - - - - - - - -
- - - - - - - - - - - - - - - - - -
- - - - - - - - - - - - - - - - - -
- - - - - - - - - - - - - - - - - -
- - - - - - - - - - - - - - - - - -
- - - - - - - - - - - - - - - - - -
- - - - - - - - - - - - - - - - - -
- - - - - - - - - - - - - - - - - -
- - - - - - - - - - - - - - - - - -
- - - - - - - - - - - - - - - - - -
- - - - - - - - - - - - - - - - - -

I FORGIVE

I WANT
TO FEEL

NOTES & EPIPHANIES

- -
- -
- -
- -
- -
- -
- -
- -

VISIONS & GUIDES

SPELL FOR

MAKING DREAMS REALITY

Your waking life is an outpicturing of your internal world,
and so is your dream state. Often, your dream state will show you
much more exaggerated representations of your current state of mind
and being, amplifying subtle or subconscious beliefs, fears or emotions.

Beyond the symbolism of the objects or events in your dreams, the
feelings you feel while these things are taking place are the true key
to unlocking the messages from the dream world. Pay attention to
how you feel in your dreams; they are showing how you feel deep down.

instructions

1. Set your intention for how you want to feel in your dream.

2. Upon waking, write down what events you can remember.

3. Note how you felt in your dream.

4. Now, do the same thing for your waking life. Before getting out of
bed, set your intention. When the day is done, journal the main events,
and write how you felt. Did you notice the power of your intention?

FURTHER READING

THE ART OF DREAMING BY CARLOS CASTENADA

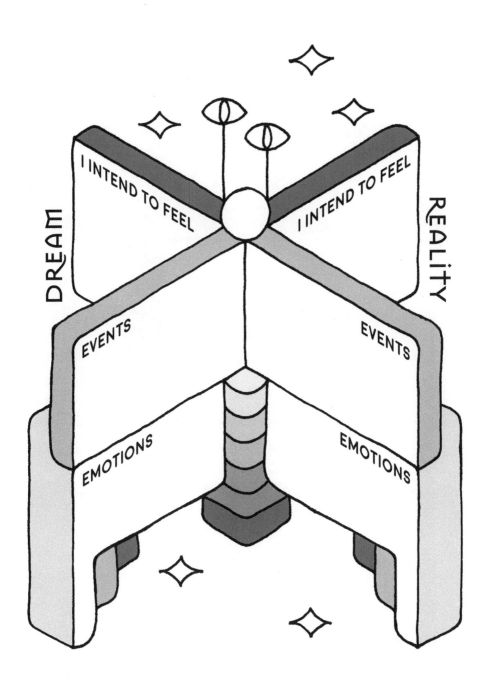

DATE • • • • • • • DREAM

QUESTION TIME

MOON PHASE
●◑◑◑○◐◑◐

ANSWERS

ANSWERS

ANSWERS

CAST A
SPELL
I'M SWITCHING TO THE VERSION
OF REALITY I PREFER. IN THE
REALITY I PREFER...

PRE-PAVE • • • • EVENT TITLE

8

BEFORE DURING AFTER

I INTEND

I PRAY

I LOVE

GRATITUDE IN ADVANCE

I'M SO GRATEFUL

I FORGIVE

I WANT TO FEEL

NOTES & EPIPHANIES

VISIONS & GUIDES

SPELL FOR

GOOD ADVICE

Do you need some solid advice to take your endeavors to the next level? A therapist, guru, life coach, or mentor can uplift and inspire positive change deliberately and consistently. But what if you need the advice right now, or don't have a guide to call on? It's time to use your imagination and your mental collection of heroes.

You have access to infinite intelligence at all times, but sometimes we need a human conduit to make the information accessible. All people know all things at all times, but answering specific questions requires allowing and remembering. And who better to help you remember than a leader you already look up to?

The following channeling process taps into universal wisdom through the voices of people you admire. You may be surprised how much help is already inside you!

instructions

1. What do you need advice about? Write down the question in the central diamond.

2. In the circles provided, write the names of six different people whose advice you would treasure. They can be living or dead, existing in celebrity or obscurity. All that matters is that you trust their perspective and opinion.

3. Now, close your eyes and imagine having a conversation with each person. Ask them the question you have written down. And then quiet your mind and wait for them to speak. Write down their advice in the corresponding rectangles next to their names.

Now you know what to do!

FURTHER READING

THINK AND GROW RICH BY NAPOLEON HILL

DATE

DREAM

QUESTION

TIME

MOON PHASE

ANSWERS

ANSWERS

ANSWERS

CAST A
SPELL

I'M SWITCHING TO THE VERSION
OF REALITY I PREFER. IN THE
REALITY I PREFER...

PRE-PAVE

EVENT TITLE

BEFORE

DURING

AFTER

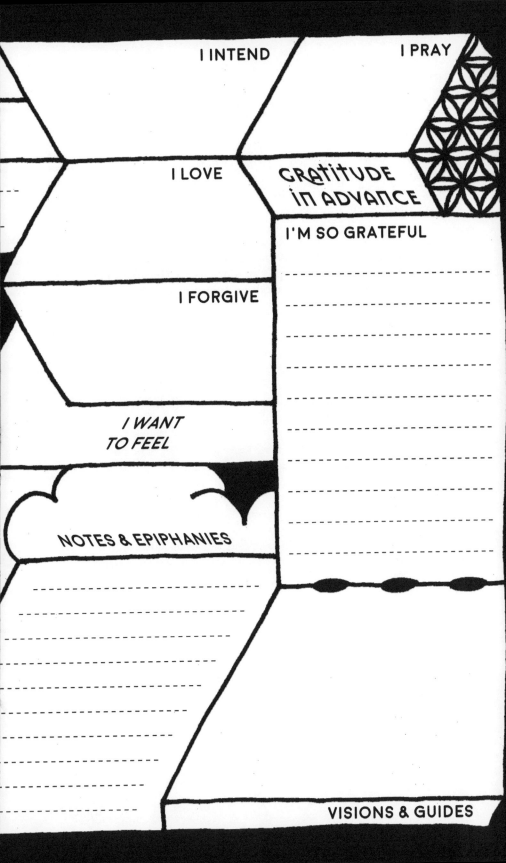

SPELL FOR

CALMING ANXIETY

A potent indicator of alignment is your breath. We try to force things into being all day long; meanwhile our breath is breathing itself in the background. Our hearts stay beating without our interference. Life is always living us, not the other way around.

In this exercise, notice your breath but don't try to control it. Observe it, don't force it. Notice when it is coming in by writing, "Breathing in, I know I am breathing in," in the space provided. Write, "Breathing out, I know I am breathing out," as you exhale. Appreciate how the breath breathes you. Continue to watch this process and write along with it until the page is full.

Now you are equipped to face your day with the knowledge that everything in life is unfolding as naturally as your breath. You're not in charge, so you can just observe. You don't have to get involved or make anything happen. You can watch from above, instead of being tossed about by the ups and downs of life.

It's all written in the breath. Life as we know it is a series of polarities: on and off, in and out, light and dark. It is this duality we came to frolic in and explore. But when you're in an ebb in life and want to get back to the flow, return to this breath mantra to help you remember what you know. When you know what you don't want, you know what you do want. The opposite of your experience is already created, and you can use your breath to guide you to that opposite side of the wave. From anxiety to tranquility, your breath is your constant connection to source.

On a scale of 1-10, rate how anxious you are before and after completing this exercise. Did it help?

BEFORE [   ]   AFTER [   ]

FURTHER READING

HOW TO RELAX BY THICH NHAT HANH

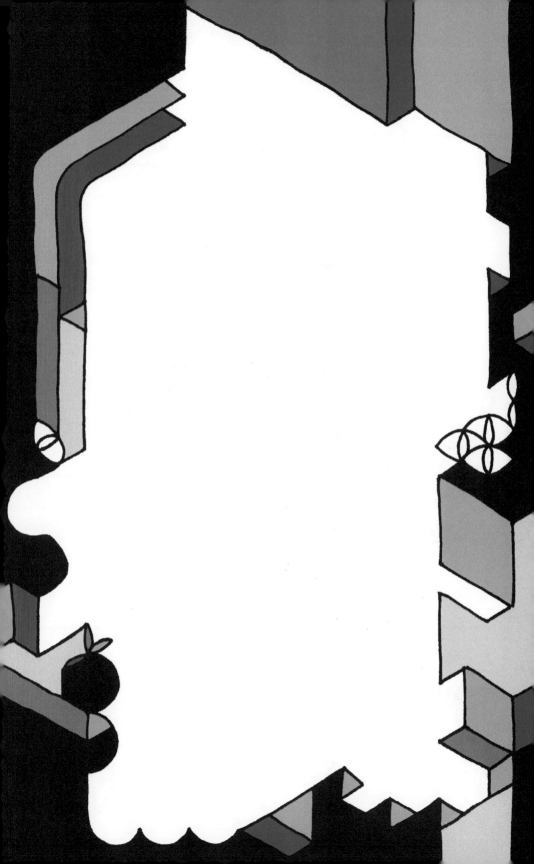

DATE

DREAM

QUESTION

TIME

MOON PHASE

●●●◐○○○◑●●

ANSWERS

ANSWERS

ANSWERS

CAST A
SPELL

I'M SWITCHING TO THE VERSION OF REALITY I PREFER. IN THE REALITY I PREFER...

PRE-PAVE

EVENT TITLE

BEFORE

DURING

AFTER

I INTEND

I PRAY

I LOVE

GRatitUDE
in ADVAnCE

I'M SO GRATEFUL

I FORGIVE

I WANT
TO FEEL

NOTES & EPIPHANIES

VISIONS & GUIDES

SPELL FOR
infinite ABUNDANCE

"Giving is an esoteric science that never fails to produce results if it is done with love and joy, because the Law will shower you with a multiplied return. But if you tithe (and I really prefer the word 'sharing' to tithing) as a mechanical and calculated method to please God, unload guilt, meet a sense of obligation, and play a bartering game with the Law, no one benefits, not even the receiver. Give with love, joy, and a sense of fun, and the windows of heaven will be thrown open with a blast!" JOHN RANDOLPH PRICE

Money (or how much you have of it), like everything else in the material world, is an indicator of your connection to source—an outpicturing of your inner world. Most people think that they will get money and then feel fulfilled but the reality is that first you must feel fulfilled and then you will attract money. Money is an indicator of well being, not a source of it.

That's why the science of giving, as John Randolph Price puts it in his book *The Abundance Book,* works so well. When you give with the knowledge that there is always more than enough and your supply isn't limited by giving it away, the "Law" responds with more. When you understand that the gifts life has for you are limitless, then they are.

instructions
Give something away today. Whether it be your time, your money, your praise or maybe your energy, give it as if there is no limit to your supply. Give it joyfully knowing that you are lucky enough to have tapped into infinite abundance. Give knowing that everything you give to life, it gives back to you (and then some). But don't do it to get something, do it for the sheer joy of sharing the infinite. How does it feel?

FURTHER READING

THE 40-DAY PROSPERITY PLAN BY JOHN RANDOLPH PRICE

TODAY I GAVE

_____

_____

_____

_____

IT FELT

_____

_____

_____

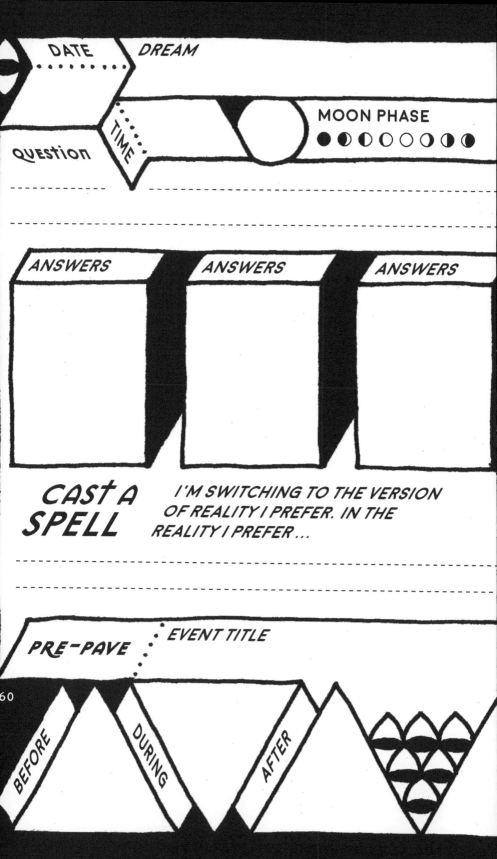

DATE

DREAM

QUESTION

TIME

MOON PHASE

ANSWERS

ANSWERS

ANSWERS

CAST A
SPELL

I'M SWITCHING TO THE VERSION
OF REALITY I PREFER. IN THE
REALITY I PREFER...

PRE-PAVE

EVENT TITLE

BEFORE

DURING

AFTER

I INTEND

I PRAY

I LOVE

GRATITUDE
IN ADVANCE

I'M SO GRATEFUL

I FORGIVE

I WANT
TO FEEL

NOTES & EPIPHANIES

VISIONS & GUIDES

SPELL FOR
HARNESSING ENERGY

"Being busy is a form of laziness—lazy thinking
and indiscriminate action." TIM FERRISS

Pareto's law states that 80% of output results from 20% of the input; for example, 80% of your income comes from 20% of your work. Imagine if you could identify the 20% of your efforts that create 80% of the desired results in your life. How free would you feel if you could cut out 80% of your activities that don't really contribute much to your well being?

When you do less, you can emphasize quality over quantity and be very deliberate about where you place your attention. Where are you placing your energy, and how much is bringing satisfaction?

instructions
In the space provided, write down everything you do in a day. Next to each half hour entry, rate the activity on a scale of 1 to 5 stars. One star means it didn't bring you much joy or value, and 5 stars means you were thrilled and satisfied.

After you complete your record for a day, look back at your ratings and evaluate how you spend your time. What would you rather do more of? And what can you cut out completely? The magick of this exercise is simple awareness. When you become conscious of your energy, it's much easier to harness, direct and enjoy.

What would you rather do more of?

What can you cut out completely?

FURTHER READING

THE 4-HOUR WORKWEEK BY TIM FERRISS

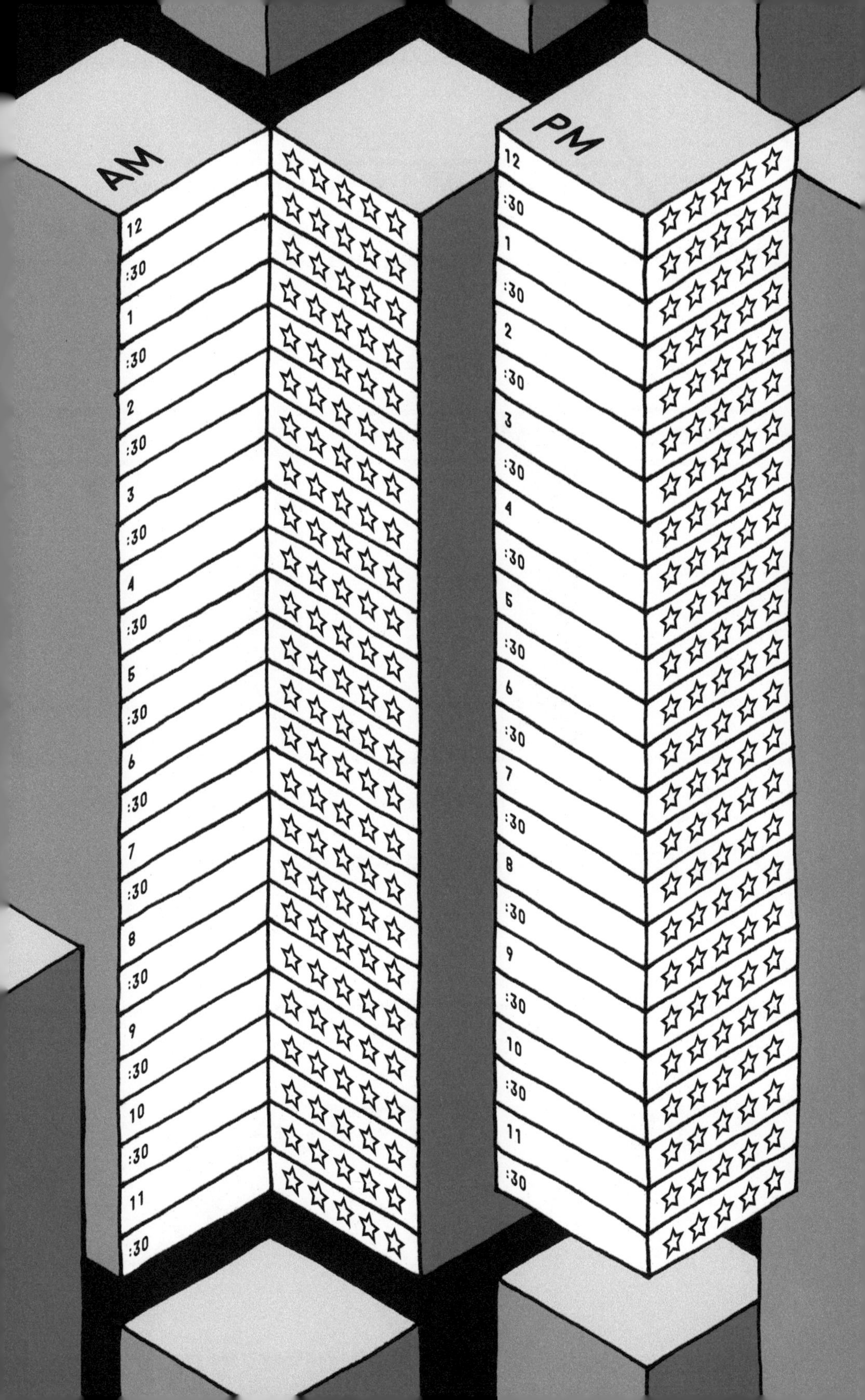
AM
12
:30
1
:30
2
:30
3
:30
4
:30
5
:30
6
:30
7
:30
8
:30
9
:30
10
:30
11
:30
PM
12
:30
1
:30
2
:30
3
:30
4
:30
5
:30
6
:30
7
:30
8
:30
9
:30
10
:30
11
:30

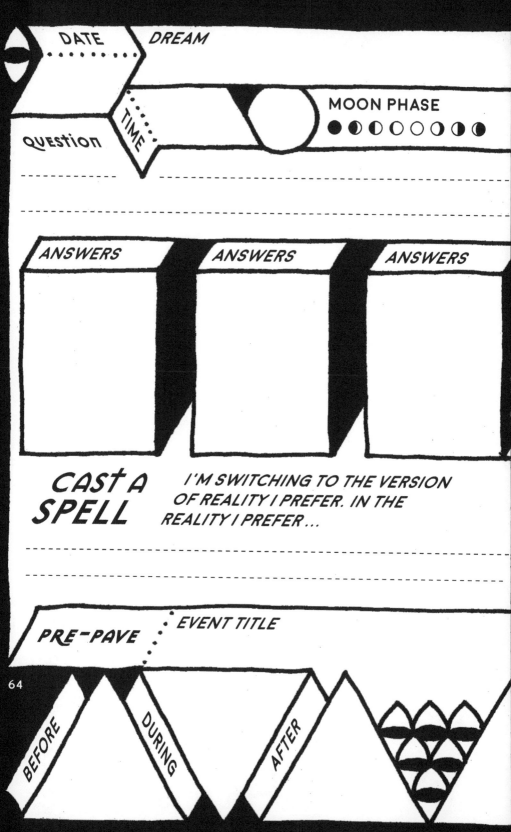

DATE

DREAM

TIME

QUESTION

MOON PHASE

ANSWERS

ANSWERS

ANSWERS

CAST A
SPELL

I'M SWITCHING TO THE VERSION
OF REALITY I PREFER. IN THE
REALITY I PREFER...

PRE-PAVE

EVENT TITLE

BEFORE

DURING

AFTER

I INTEND

I PRAY

I LOVE

GRATITUDE
IN ADVANCE

I'M SO GRATEFUL

I FORGIVE

I WANT
TO FEEL

NOTES & EPIPHANIES

VISIONS & GUIDES

SPELL FOR

TRANSCENDENCE

There is an aspect of you that thinks thoughts. It judges and resists everything around you. It decides yes or no, right or wrong. There is also an aspect of you that witnesses those thoughts—your higher self.

When we forget to observe our thoughts from the perspective of our higher selves, we can start to believe that we ARE our thoughts and even worse—that our thoughts are "true." When we are identified with these thoughts, we follow them. We expend a lot of our energy wondering about what ifs. However, when we zoom out and notice the thoughts (and notice the noticing), we realize we don't have to chase every thought that passes through. When we simply watch our thoughts instead of follow them down rabbit holes, we can bring lasting peace to our lives.

Use the process below to embody your observer self. Notice that simply becoming aware of this perspective will bring forth a sense of calm bliss. Next time something bothers you, rather than get wrapped up in the event, assume the observer perspective and see what kind of insights this awareness can bring to the situation.

instructions

1. Draw an abstract representation of what your thoughts look like in your mind.

2. When you imagined your thoughts in your mind just now, who or what was doing the observing?

3. From where are the thoughts being observed?

4. How does this perspective feel?

5. Now that you have changed your point of view to observer, take a look at your thoughts again. Do the thoughts slow down? Do they fall into a beautiful formation? Draw a visual representation of your energy after working through this process.

FURTHER READING

THE BOOK: ON THE TABOO AGAINST KNOWING WHO YOU ARE BY ALAN WATTS

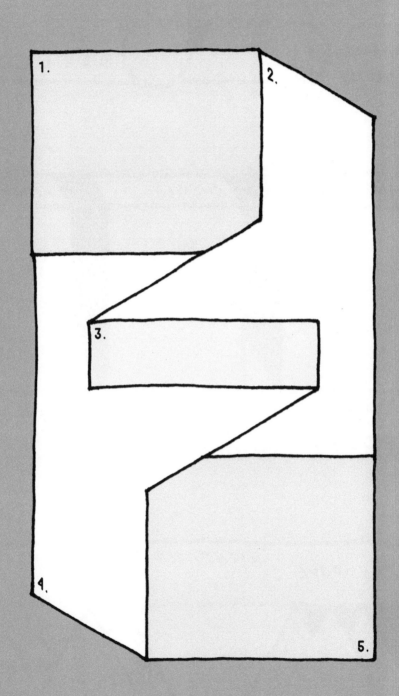

DATE

DREAM

MOON PHASE
●◐◑◑○◑◑●

QUESTION

TIME

ANSWERS

ANSWERS

ANSWERS

CAST A SPELL

I'M SWITCHING TO THE VERSION OF REALITY I PREFER. IN THE REALITY I PREFER...

PRE-PAVE

EVENT TITLE

BEFORE

DURING

AFTER

I INTEND

I PRAY

I LOVE

GRATITUDE
IN ADVANCE

I'M SO GRATEFUL

I FORGIVE

I WANT
TO FEEL

NOTES & EPIPHANIES

VISIONS & GUIDES

SPELL FOR
WEIGHTLESSNESS

The things we don't like about other people can help us see where we need to forgive ourselves. When we notice someone else's shortcomings, it is an indicator of what we dislike in our own selves. When we berate someone for being careless, we are calling ourselves out for our own past error. We wouldn't notice the negative behavior if it hadn't first originated in ourselves.

We feel guilty for the things we don't like about ourselves. But often the things we don't like lie below our surface of consciousness. It's easy to notice flaws in others, but a little more difficult to see those same flaws in ourselves. But as the old adage goes, "It takes one to know one."

When you see something you don't like in someone, embrace this opportunity to forgive yourself. If you can truly forgive yourself for the same egregious behavior, you won't be bothered by it in someone else. By giving yourself the love and forgiveness you crave, you also offer it to the person reflecting you. With forgiveness comes freedom, and the delight of a weight lifted!

instructions

1. What is a grudge you're holding? Write the person's name and what the grudge is for.

2. If your grudge had a weight, how much would it weigh?

3. Write down a time when you remember yourself doing the same thing you're begrudging.

4. Forgive yourself for this heinous act by completing the sentence, "I forgive myself for..."

5. Now transfer that forgiveness to the person who hurt you. Finish the sentence, "I also forgive..." with the person's name.

6. Now you can see you were both in need of help and healing. Do you feel a weight lifted? How much does your grudge weigh now?

FURTHER READING

DAILY MEDITATIONS FOR PRACTICING THE COURSE BY KAREN CASEY

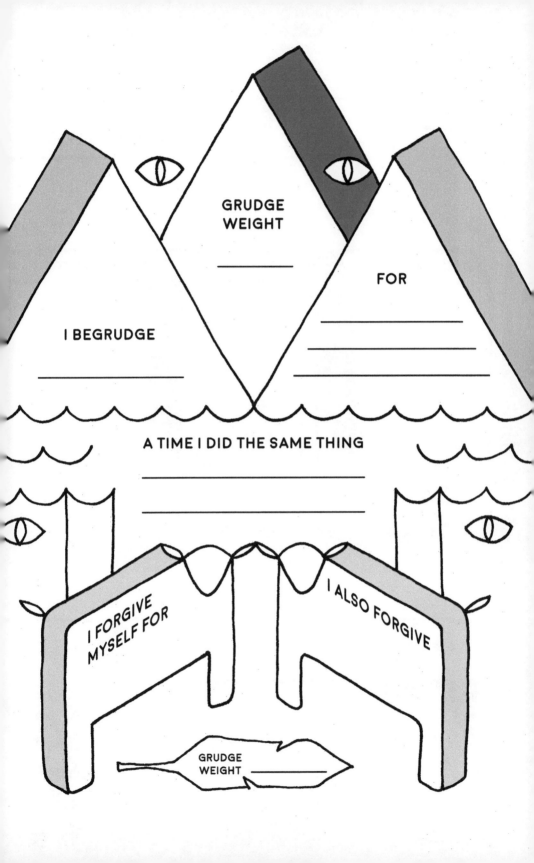

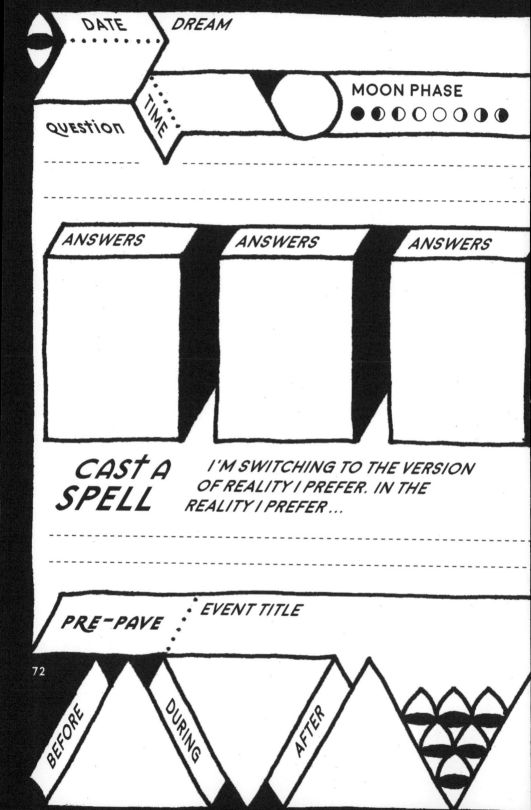

DATE

DREAM

QUESTION

TIME

MOON PHASE

ANSWERS   ANSWERS   ANSWERS

CAST A
SPELL

I'M SWITCHING TO THE VERSION
OF REALITY I PREFER. IN THE
REALITY I PREFER...

PRE-PAVE

EVENT TITLE

BEFORE   DURING   AFTER

I INTEND

I PRAY

I LOVE

GRATITUDE
IN ADVANCE

I'M SO GRATEFUL

- -
- -
- -

I FORGIVE

- -
- -
- -
- -
- -

*I WANT
TO FEEL*

- -
- -

NOTES & EPIPHANIES

- -
- -
- -
- -
- -
- -
- -
- -
- -
- -

VISIONS & GUIDES

SPELL FOR

POWER

Your power comes from your presence. When your attention is focused in the thin slice of NOW between the past and future, you have access to divine inspiration, your intuition, and universal intelligence. In the present moment, play becomes possible. In the present moment, your manifesting abilities are at their peak, because you aren't resisting the natural flow of well being with your thoughts.

Silent counting is a technique for becoming present. It is the practice of consciously focusing on a stream of numbers in your head, instead of following the whirlwind trains of thought trying to scatter your attention. All day, every day, we are barraged with thoughts that can take our imaginations into the darkness. But silent counting gives us a way to remain present in the moment during our daily activities. Use silent counting to plug the attention drain of scattered thinking and charge your magickal power back up.

instructions
Count each box on the next page. Write numbers in the boxes, color them or draw dots in each shape. Keep count of your penstrokes in your mind. Try to reach 100, then start over. Aim to count to 10,000 in one day for supreme focus and empowerment.

FURTHER READING

THE POWER OF NOW BY ECKHART TOLLE

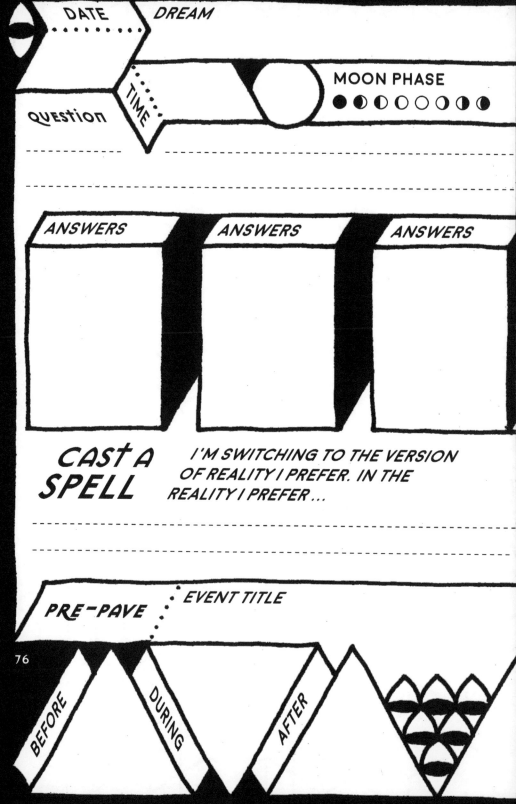

DATE

DREAM

QUESTION

TIME

MOON PHASE

ANSWERS

ANSWERS

ANSWERS

CAST A
SPELL

I'M SWITCHING TO THE VERSION
OF REALITY I PREFER. IN THE
REALITY I PREFER...

PRE-PAVE

EVENT TITLE

BEFORE

DURING

AFTER

I INTEND

I PRAY

I LOVE

GRATITUDE
IN ADVANCE

I'M SO GRATEFUL

I FORGIVE

I WANT
TO FEEL

NOTES & EPIPHANIES

VISIONS & GUIDES

SPELL FOR
LETTING GO

In his book *The Surrender Experiment*, Michael Singer tells the story of the incredible amount of success he achieved in his life simply by saying yes to everything that came his way. At one point, a woman decides to build a home (!) on his property. While he was admittedly upset at first, he eventually surrendered and helped her build the house. On his own property! It turned out that he loved building the house, so much so that he later started his own wildly successful home-building company.

Life is always giving us gifts. Constantly. All day, every day. And most of the time, we look at the gifts thinking, "Not what I wanted," or "Thanks, but no thanks," or "Hell no, send this back!" However, when we begin graciously accepting everything that comes our way, we lift the veil on the illusion. We start seeing everything in life is happening for us, not to us.

Fill the frame with the word "Yes." This exercise will help get your mind running on that track and put your surrender on auto-pilot. Anything that happens, say yes. Return to this page at the end of the day and write down one thing you said yes to and how it affected your day.

One thing I said yes to:

_____

How it affected my day:

_____

FURTHER READING

THE SURRENDER EXPERIMENT BY MICHAEL SINGER

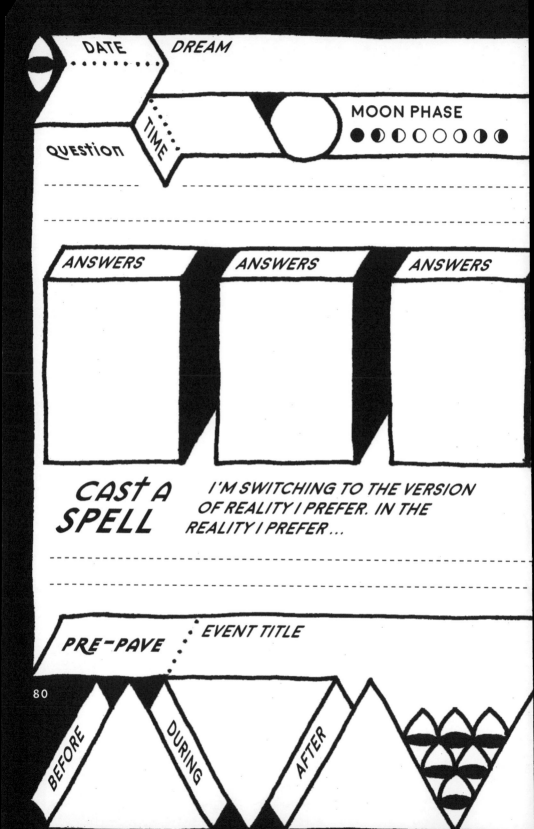

DATE

DREAM

QUESTION

TIME

MOON PHASE

ANSWERS

ANSWERS

ANSWERS

CAST A SPELL

I'M SWITCHING TO THE VERSION OF REALITY I PREFER. IN THE REALITY I PREFER...

PRE-PAVE

EVENT TITLE

BEFORE

DURING

AFTER

I INTEND

I PRAY

I LOVE

GRATITUDE
IN ADVANCE

I'M SO GRATEFUL

- -

- -

I FORGIVE

- -

- -

- -

- -

*I WANT
TO FEEL*

- -

- -

NOTES & EPIPHANIES

- -

- -

- -

- -

- -

- -

- -

- -

VISIONS & GUIDES

DETACHMENT

Have you ever noticed that when you haven't thought much about wanting something, it can be a lot easier to manifest than the things you've wanted and wanted and wanted? That's often because there exist deeper, more ingrained vibrations about the desire not being fulfilled. Your mind may be telling you, "You've wanted this for a long time and it still hasn't come; you're probably never going to get it." Or maybe you've built up so much awareness around the not having of it that it's hard for you to believe it's possible to have at all. Today, take your stale desire and release it for good with sigil magick.

instructions

1. Convert your deepest desire into a pictogram using the symbolic alphabet provided. Be sure not to write the desire in letters anywhere. You don't want to see the word(s) on the page, only the symbols. Your desire should be phrased as if you already have it, so if you want more friends, start with, "I have so many new friends." As you convert the desire into pictures, skip vowels and repeated letters.

2. Now, conjure the feeling of what it will feel like when this desire is fulfilled. Focus on feeling the feeling deeply. Don't get too lost in visualizing the *how*, rather stay centered in the emotion this manifestation brings about. Describe the feeling in the space provided.

Your desire is no longer a boulder in your gut that just keeps getting heavier. You've converted it to mere shapes and symbols and released it to the universe. Either it's on its way or you never needed it. Either way, you can choose to feel the feeling you wrote down any time you think about it. And sooner or later, the feeling of having it will replace the perception that you don't.

FURTHER READING

MAGICK: LIBER ABA, BOOK 4 BY ALEISTER CROWLEY

DATE **DREAM**

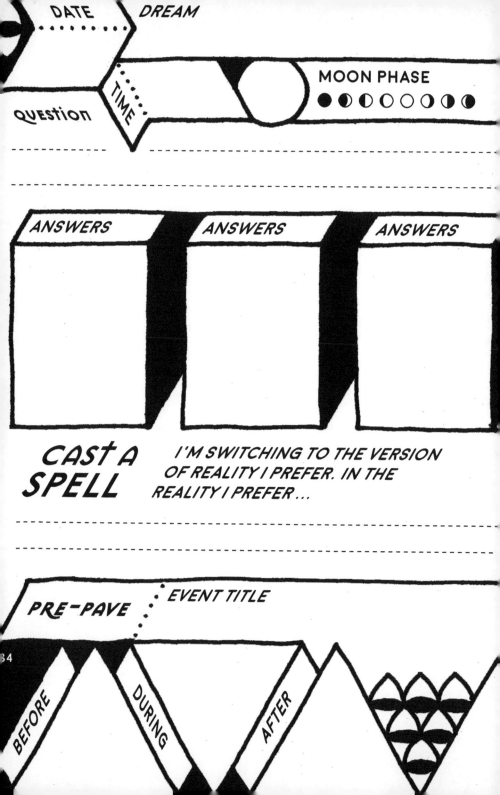

QUESTION   TIME

MOON PHASE
● ◐ ◑ ◒ ○ ◓ ◔ ◗

- - - - - - - -   - - - - - - - - - - - - - - - - - -

- -

ANSWERS   ANSWERS   ANSWERS

CAST A
SPELL

I'M SWITCHING TO THE VERSION
OF REALITY I PREFER. IN THE
REALITY I PREFER...

- -

- -

PRE-PAVE   EVENT TITLE

BEFORE   DURING   AFTER

I INTEND

I PRAY

I LOVE

GRATITUDE IN ADVANCE

I'M SO GRATEFUL

I FORGIVE

I WANT
TO FEEL

NOTES & EPIPHANIES

VISIONS & GUIDES

SPELL FOR
THRIVING

Timothy Leary was an American psychologist and writer known for advocating for therapeutic use of LSD and other psychedelics. He popularized the phrase "Turn on, tune in, drop out" in 1966 to encourage people to welcome cultural change with the help of psychedelics. Turning on meant becoming sensitive to different levels of consciousness. Tuning in meant to exist in harmony with the world. And dropping out meant to think for oneself and extricate oneself from hierarchies or institutions that one had involuntarily or unconsciously participated in.

We can get a glimpse of the magick of psychedelics with just a few words of intention. Knowing that consciousness, harmony and free thinking are possible, we can choose them for ourselves right now. We can be the change we wish to see in the world by turning on, tuning in and dropping out.

instructions

1. What are you conscious of? Is it your breathing, your surroundings, your thoughts, your body, or maybe a particularly potent truth? What are you aware of in this very moment?

2. What do you want to live in harmony with? Use this opportunity to contribute to a more peaceful planet, home life or inner world.

3. What system, institution or hierarchy have you unwillingly or unknowingly participated in, that you wish to step away from? The oil industry, politics, or maybe specific grooming habits? What have you been conditioned to do that is no longer serving you? Make the choice to step away right now and begin creating your own system of thriving.

FURTHER READING

TURN ON, TUNE IN, DROP OUT BY TIMOTHY LEARY
YOUR BRAIN IS GOD BY TIMOTHY LEARY

DATE DREAM

QUESTION TIME

MOON PHASE
●◐◑◐○◐◑◐●

ANSWERS ANSWERS ANSWERS

CAST A
SPELL

I'M SWITCHING TO THE VERSION
OF REALITY I PREFER. IN THE
REALITY I PREFER...

PRE-PAVE EVENT TITLE

BEFORE DURING AFTER

I INTEND

I PRAY

I LOVE

GRATITUDE
IN ADVANCE

I'M SO GRATEFUL

I FORGIVE

----

*I WANT
TO FEEL*

NOTES & EPIPHANIES

VISIONS & GUIDES

SPELL FOR
UПBLOCKIПG EПERGY

When you have a serious problem plaguing you, turn to chakra visualization. Your chakras are seven energy centers in your body, through which your life force flows. When you have a blocked chakra, you may notice physical symptoms in your body, or experience related problems in your life experience. But it's a simple fix to get your energy flowing smoothly again.

Since your chakras are invisible, visualization is an easy way to "speak" to them. When you have a specific problem you'd like solved, go within, light up your chakras, and get the energy flowing again.

instructions

Set your intention. What do you want? Phrase your desire with gratitude in advance. For example, if you want a cure for a health problem, your intention can be, "Thank you for healing me." Whatever it is you want, think to yourself, "Thank you for _____," as if it has already happened, and write it in the space provided.

Visualize a ball of white light coming in through your crown chakra. Send this ball of light through all your chakras (crown, third eye, throat, heart, solar plexus, navel, and tailbone), lighting up each energy center from top to bottom. This balances the energy in your body and makes you a clear conduit. Try thinking, "Breathing in, I bring light into my crown chakra. Breathing out I activate my crown chakra," and so on for each energy center.

Once your chakras are all lit up, spend a couple minutes feeling that energy flow while you focus on your intention. "Thank you for healing me. Thank you for healing me."

After your visualization, ground the energy by saying, "I ground this energy that hasn't been used. I return it to the earth. Thank you for helping me." Repeat this process 15 minutes a day for maximum results.

FURTHER READIПG

MAKING MAGICK BY EDAIN MCCOY

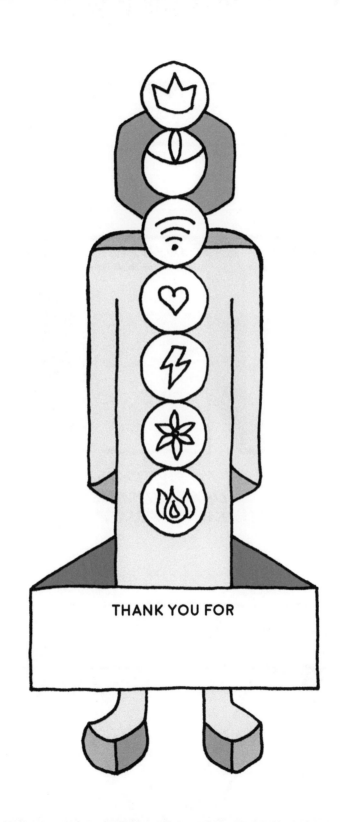

THANK YOU FOR

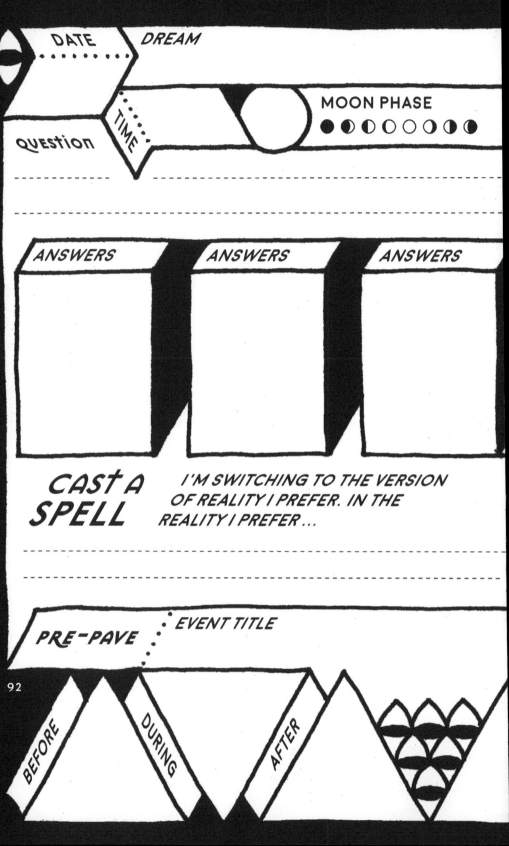

DATE .... DREAM

MOON PHASE
● ◑ ◑ ◐ ○ ◐ ◑ ◑

QUESTION   TIME

ANSWERS   ANSWERS   ANSWERS

CAST A SPELL   I'M SWITCHING TO THE VERSION OF REALITY I PREFER. IN THE REALITY I PREFER...

PRE-PAVE   EVENT TITLE

BEFORE   DURING   AFTER

I INTEND

I PRAY

I LOVE

GRATITUDE
IN ADVANCE

I'M SO GRATEFUL

I FORGIVE

I WANT
TO FEEL

NOTES & EPIPHANIES

VISIONS & GUIDES

SPELL FOR

VALIDATION

Do you ever notice yourself caring a little too much about Instagram likes? Or maybe you really want your parents to support your choices? The need for external validation comes as a result of feeling ashamed of ourselves. We feel like we don't measure up to someone else's standards. Maybe we feel like we haven't achieved enough yet or made enough money. When we feel ashamed, we think that praise from other people will help us feel better. But it never will until we address the root of the problem: our shame.

There's no need for deep psychological unearthing to get to the bottom of this. Use a simple pivoting process to start noticing (and switching to) the opposite side of the energetic wave. The opposite of shame is pride, and you can choose to feel proud of yourself right now.

When we deliberately choose to feel proud of ourselves, we start noticing the things we do that we truly are proud of. Getting out of bed, being kind to a stranger, eating a vegetable—there are so many tiny acts we perform each day to be proud of. Today, let, "I'm so proud of myself" be your mantra. Before long, you will start liking yourself so much that you won't need to hear it from anyone else.

instructions
Fill the frame with the words, "I am so proud of myself." Try to really feel the emotion of pride in yourself as you're writing. Notice how empowering it feels to be proud of yourself.

Note one thing you noticed you are proud of yourself for after doing this exercise:

FURTHER READING

MONEY AND THE LAW OF ATTRACTION BY ESTHER AND JERRY HICKS

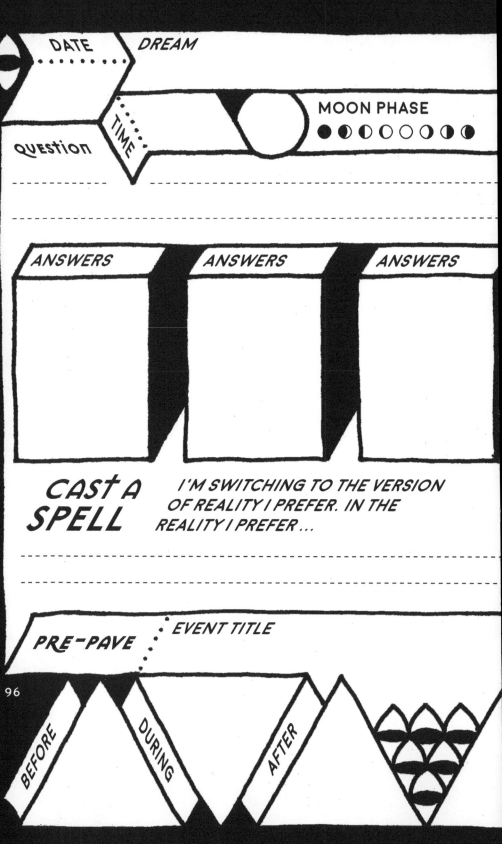

DATE · · · · · · · DREAM

TIME

QUESTION

MOON PHASE
●◐◑◒○○○◐◑

ANSWERS

ANSWERS

ANSWERS

CAST A SPELL

I'M SWITCHING TO THE VERSION OF REALITY I PREFER. IN THE REALITY I PREFER...

PRE-PAVE · · · · EVENT TITLE

BEFORE

DURING

AFTER

I INTEND

I PRAY

I LOVE

GRATITUDE
IN ADVANCE

I'M SO GRATEFUL

I FORGIVE

----

*I WANT
TO FEEL*

NOTES & EPIPHANIES

VISIONS & GUIDES

SPELL FOR

∏⊙∏-ACTI⊙∏

Force, by definition, implies action. One thing is acting upon another, and there's usually some resistance involved. If something is easy, you're not forcing it. It slides right into place; it doesn't require energy.

The opposite of force is ease, and as the *Tao Te Ching* by Lao Tzu explains, "The Tao does nothing, but leaves nothing left undone." The energy that creates worlds is flowing through you. It doesn't need you to interfere in its plan. Notice how when you get out of the way and don't meddle in the happenings of your life, more happens easier, faster and without complication than when you try to hammer things into place.

For example, say you want upper body strength. If you were forcing it, you might create a rigid workout schedule, go on a diet, and spend hours researching how to improve your form. But if you were allowing upper body strength to come to you, maybe you would start rock climbing for fun. You get so into rock climbing that one day you realize you've been pulling yourself up by your arms, not even noticing that now you have the upper body strength you desired. What if what you wanted to achieve came as a by-product of doing something fun? Let this exercise open your mind to the possibilities of allowing instead of forcing, and see what unfolds.

instructions
Write down something you want to achieve, but have been struggling with. In the block of ice, write what it would look like to try to force it to happen. What kinds of action do you have to take? How does it feel?

Now, imagine allowing your achievement into existence. In the water below the ice, write what fun things might lead you to your achievement, if you were allowing life to flow. How does it feel to allow instead of force?

FURTHER READING

TAO TE CHING BY LAO TZU

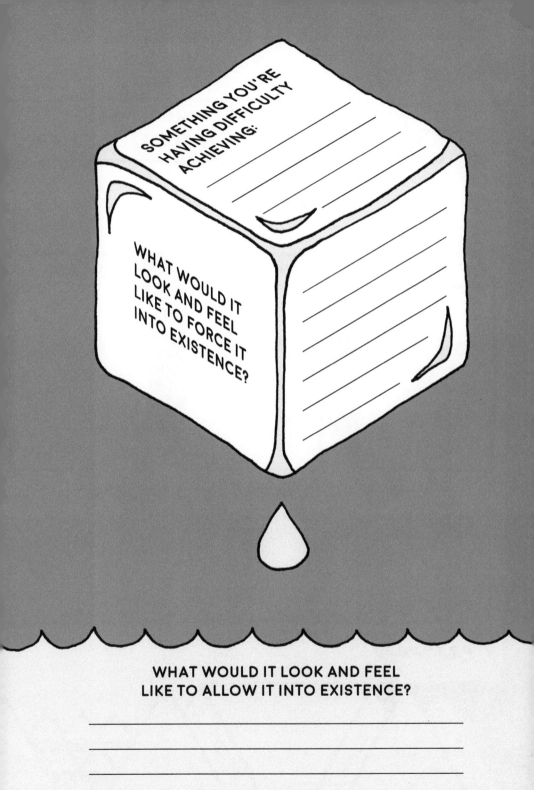

SOMETHING YOU'RE HAVING DIFFICULTY ACHIEVING:

WHAT WOULD IT LOOK AND FEEL LIKE TO FORCE IT INTO EXISTENCE?

WHAT WOULD IT LOOK AND FEEL LIKE TO ALLOW IT INTO EXISTENCE?

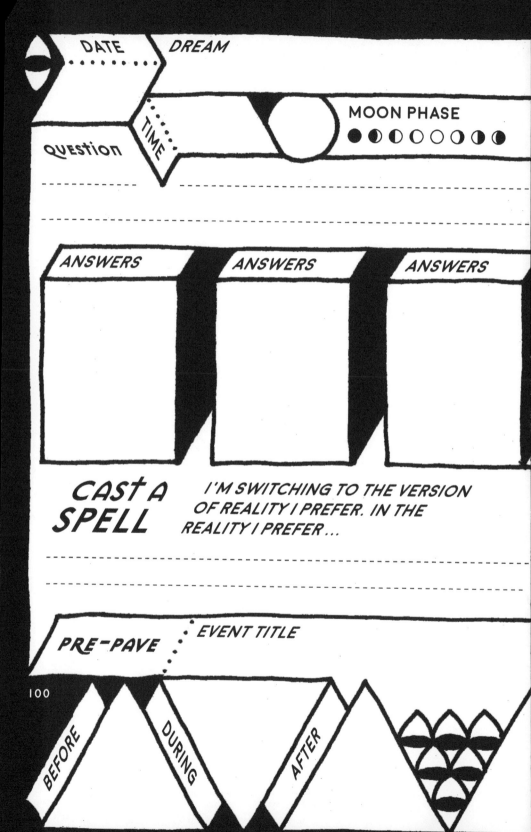

DATE

DREAM

TIME

QUestion

MOON PHASE

ANSWERS

ANSWERS

ANSWERS

CAST A
SPELL

I'M SWITCHING TO THE VERSION
OF REALITY I PREFER. IN THE
REALITY I PREFER...

PRE-PAVE

EVENT TITLE

100

BEFORE

DURING

AFTER

I INTEND

I PRAY

I LOVE

GRATITUDE
IN ADVANCE

I'M SO GRATEFUL

I FORGIVE

I WANT
TO FEEL

NOTES & EPIPHANIES

VISIONS & GUIDES

SPELL FOR

APPRECIATING IN VALUE

A phrase we use often in our work is, "Even when you're saying no, you're saying yes." Influenced by the teachings of Abraham-Hicks, this means that even if you don't want something, if you are giving it attention, you attract more of it. When you focus on how much you don't want something, you create more of it in your life by giving your attention to it, because what you focus on, expands. Notice it, get more of it. What you resist, persists.

On the other hand, if you can find a way to be at peace with what nags you—even going so far as to be grateful for what you do not prefer—you will see that the thing you think is in your way is actually giving you the powerful opportunity to align with your truest and deepest desires.

instructions

Write down something you are definitely *not* grateful for in the space provided, then fill in the chart below to note your level of peace in relationship to the topic. Then come up with as many reasons as possible why you *can* be grateful for that thing, and write them in the blank rectangles. Maybe having to go to the Post Office is helping you get exercise, or maybe your neighbor's loud music is helping you not overwork yourself. How peaceful do you feel now? Record it below.

BEFORE   AFTER

When you're able to shift your focus to things that you *are* grateful for, you'll notice that what you once thought was a problem is presenting you with a solution.

FURTHER READING

ASK AND IT IS GIVEN BY ESTHER AND JERRY HICKS

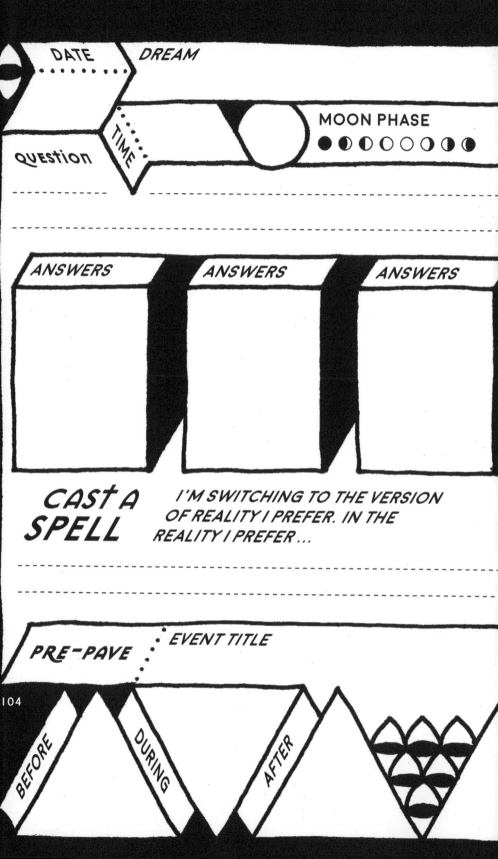

DATE ········ DREAM

QUESTION ··· TIME

MOON PHASE
● ◐ ◑ ◑ ○ ○ ○ ◗ ●

ANSWERS

ANSWERS

ANSWERS

CAST A
SPELL

I'M SWITCHING TO THE VERSION
OF REALITY I PREFER. IN THE
REALITY I PREFER...

PRE-PAVE ···· EVENT TITLE

BEFORE

DURING

AFTER

I INTEND

I PRAY

I LOVE

GRATITUDE
IN ADVANCE

I'M SO GRATEFUL

I FORGIVE

I WANT
TO FEEL

NOTES & EPIPHANIES

VISIONS & GUIDES

SPELL FOR
GETTING IN THE ZONE

We all love that feeling of being so totally immersed in something that the world slips away, and all that remains is the pleasure of dancing in sync with the present moment. Runners experience this as "runners high." Performance artists use hula hoops and other props to enter that timeless world of play. Even sitting at our computers, we can get lost in the buzz of completing a task harmoniously and in perfect time.

This rhythm is known as "being in the flow," and it's easier to get there than our minds want us to believe. The trick to getting in this zone is to quiet our minds but busy our bodies. When our thoughts aren't getting in the way of our motion, we enter into the divine pulse of the universe.

You can jump back in the flow of life with a walk outside. Being outside of the comfort zone of our homes wakes us up into observer position. The movement of our bodies moves our life force energy so it doesn't stagnate in one place. The mind relaxes and opens up to new ideas. Epiphanies and a better mood inevitably ensue.

instructions
Take a walk today, or if you aren't able to walk, find a way to get your body outside and moving in the world. If you are bedridden or house-bound, take the journey in your mind.

Make a map of where you went. Note the start and end points, as well whatever good ideas, cool places, favorite parts, friends, cute or beautiful things, magick, mysteries, love or signs of abundance you noticed.

Measure your mood on a scale of 1-10 before and after your walk.

BEFORE [   ]   AFTER [   ]

FURTHER READING

FLOW BY MIHALY CSIKSZENTMIHALYI

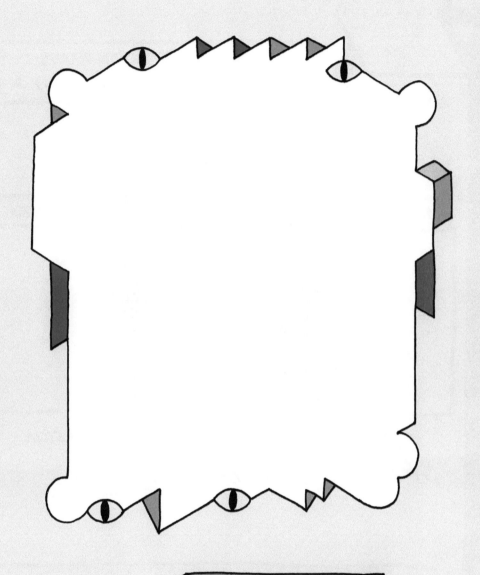

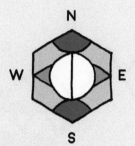

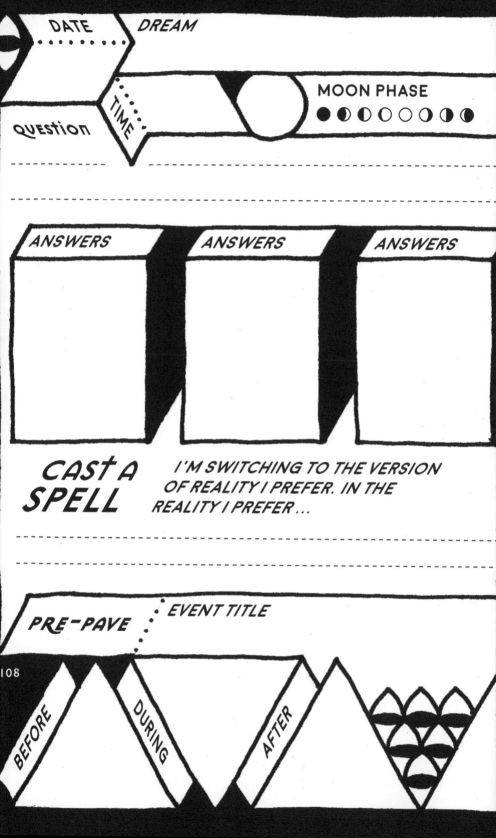

DATE

DREAM

QUESTION

TIME

MOON PHASE

ANSWERS

ANSWERS

ANSWERS

CAST A
SPELL

I'M SWITCHING TO THE VERSION
OF REALITY I PREFER. IN THE
REALITY I PREFER...

PRE-PAVE

EVENT TITLE

BEFORE

DURING

AFTER

I INTEND

I PRAY

I LOVE

GRATITUDE
IN ADVANCE

I'M SO GRATEFUL

I FORGIVE

I WANT
TO FEEL

NOTES & EPIPHANIES

VISIONS & GUIDES

SPELL FOR
ENDING SUFFERING

Nichiren Buddhism focuses heavily on the removal of oneself from the roller coaster of life's ups and downs. Rather, practitioners encourage chanting the words, "Nam Myoho Renge Kyo," which translate to "Devotion to the Mystic Law of the Lotus Sutra," or, "Devotion to the Mystic Law of Cause and Effect." Each thought is a cause that immediately creates an effect. Nichiren Buddhists believe that NMRK is the highest thought one may think, which allows the ideal outcome to manifest. When one chants NMRK, all trust is turned over to the universe: "I give up! I resign myself to the flow of life!"

Suffering always stems from attachment. It could be attachment to outcomes, people, circumstances, objects, beliefs and so on, but suffering always comes from thinking something should be different from how it is. What if we didn't need things to be different, or to be a certain way for us to be happy? What if we could be okay with how life is, because we trust the unfolding of things?

Fill the frame with the words "Nam Myoho Renge Kyo." When your mind starts to wander to that project you need to finish or that conversation you're dreading, tell your mind, "Nam Myoho Renge Kyo." As you write the words, feel how good it feels to know that this is your only responsibility now. Your only "job" is to give in.

NMRK is notorious for bringing about miracles. Be on the lookout today for pinhead solutions and major manifestions and record them below.

_____

_____

_____

_____

FURTHER READING

THE LOTUS SUTRA : A CONTEMPORARY TRANSLATION OF A BUDDHIST CLASSIC BY GENE REEVES

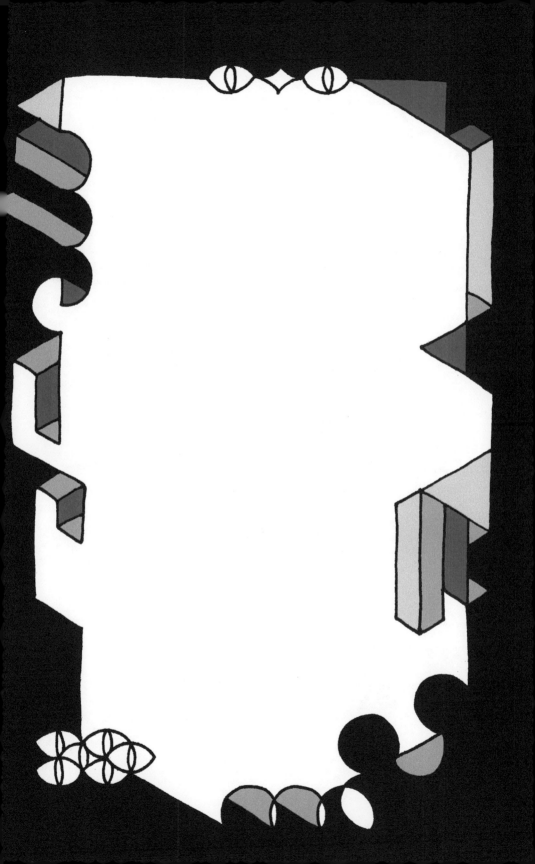

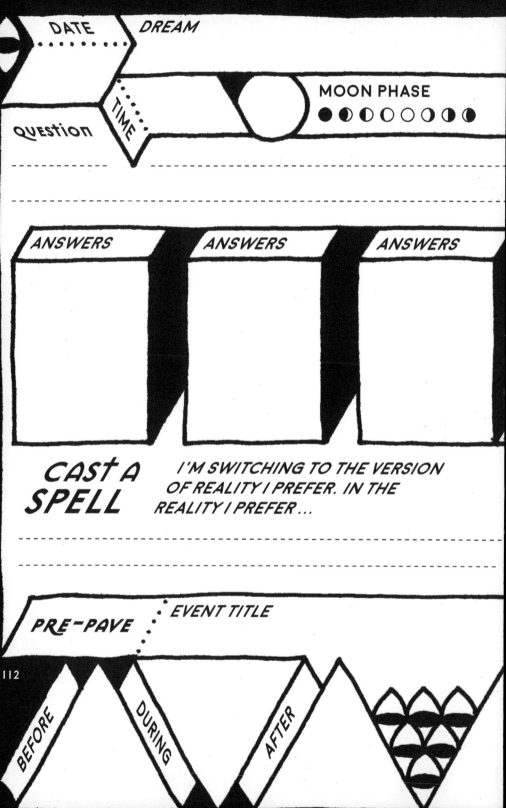

DATE

DREAM

QUESTION

TIME

MOON PHASE

ANSWERS

ANSWERS

ANSWERS

CAST A
SPELL

I'M SWITCHING TO THE VERSION
OF REALITY I PREFER. IN THE
REALITY I PREFER ...

PRE-PAVE

EVENT TITLE

BEFORE

DURING

AFTER

I INTEND

I PRAY

I LOVE

GRatitUDE
in ADVAnCE

I'M SO GRATEFUL

I FORGIVE

I WANT
TO FEEL

NOTES & EPIPHANIES

VISIONS & GUIDES

SPELL FOR

FEARLESSNESS

When we are afraid, it's usually a fear of the unknown. We "don't know" what's going to happen, and that makes us feel uncomfortable and nervous. But what if you did know? What if you knew you never had to worry? You never have to worry because everything is always responding to your inner world. When you line up the energy within, the world has no choice but to respond. Beyond that, you will feel good no matter what happens. When you make the choice to feel good no matter what happens, you don't have to be afraid because you know the outcome doesn't affect your state of being. Practice being at peace despite outcomes and you won't ever have to be afraid again.

instructions

1. Write down what you're afraid of and your fear level associated with that fear.

How can you continue living even if the worst happens?
How can you make peace? Might there even be a silver lining in the worst possible scenario?

2. Write down how you can feel good even if your (often irrational) fears come true. Now that you've made peace with what you don't want to happen, are you less afraid? Has your fear level subsided? Write down your fear level now.

FURTHER READING

THE ESSENTIAL RUMI BY RUMI

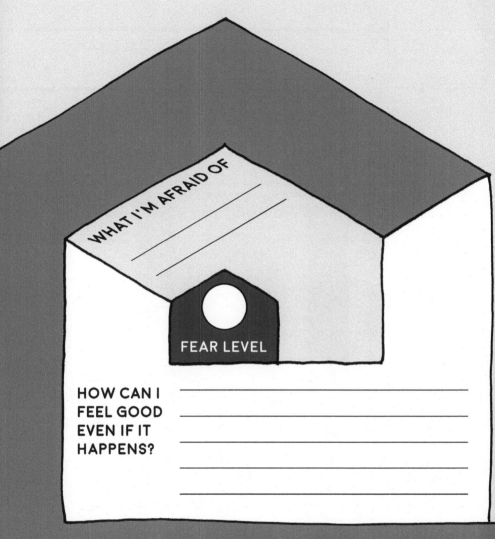

WHAT I'M AFRAID OF
_____
_____

FEAR LEVEL

HOW CAN I
FEEL GOOD
EVEN IF IT
HAPPENS?
_____
_____
_____
_____
_____

FEAR
LEVEL

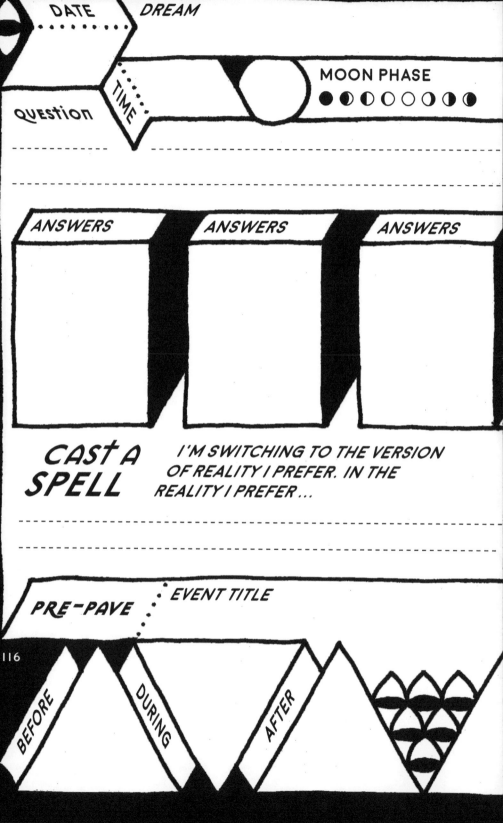

DATE DREAM

QUESTION TIME

MOON PHASE

ANSWERS ANSWERS ANSWERS

CAST A SPELL

I'M SWITCHING TO THE VERSION OF REALITY I PREFER. IN THE REALITY I PREFER...

PRE-PAVE EVENT TITLE

BEFORE DURING AFTER

I INTEND

I PRAY

I LOVE

GRATITUDE
IN ADVANCE

I'M SO GRATEFUL

I FORGIVE

I WANT
TO FEEL

NOTES & EPIPHANIES

VISIONS & GUIDES

SPELL FOR
RECEIVING

> "No offense to Napoleon Hill, the author of the self-help classic on which my
> title riffs, but the real power is in not thinking. If you want to override your
> brain's unfortunate habit of leafing through your past and creating a present
> hologram to match, forget thinking. And start thanking." PAM GROUT

Grout goes on to explain that you don't have to do anything to connect
to the energy field that attracts the most extraordinary aspects of life
besides simply tune out the voices that tell you otherwise. Replace all of
your doubts, fears and self loathing with "thank you" and you will be on
the path to miracles.

instructions
Fill the frame provided with the words "thank you." You don't even have
to be thinking about a certain object or experience that you're particularly grateful for. Just write the words "thank you." Write them over and
over again. And when your mind starts to wander to something you're
definitely not grateful for, tune it back to "thank you." Feel the
resonance that comes just from writing the words. Feel the gratitude
that flows into your being just from writing the words. And then
notice all the things you have to be grateful for that rush to your mind.
Replace all other thoughts with thank you. Write it so many times that
your thought pattern defaults to it. Then take this mantra into your day
and thank everything. Then write down the major manifestations you
allowed in your life by simply tuning out the thoughts that told you
they weren't possible.

MIRACLE LOG

_____

_____

_____

_____

FURTHER READING

THANK AND GROW RICH BY PAM GROUT

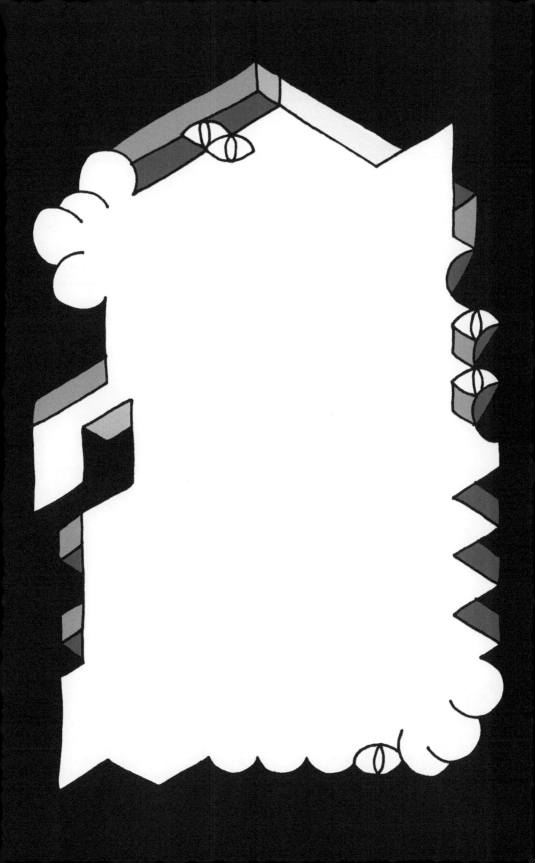

DATE DREAM

QUESTION TIME

MOON PHASE

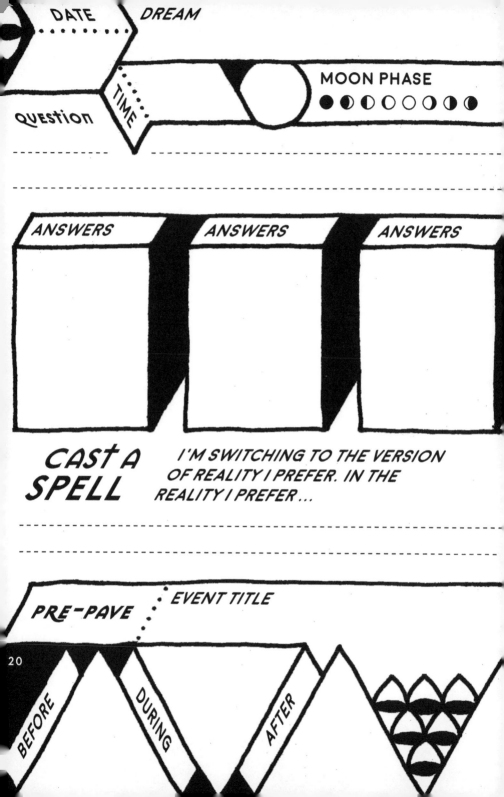

ANSWERS   ANSWERS   ANSWERS

CAST A SPELL

I'M SWITCHING TO THE VERSION OF REALITY I PREFER. IN THE REALITY I PREFER...

PRE-PAVE   EVENT TITLE

BEFORE   DURING   AFTER

I INTEND

I PRAY

I LOVE

GRATITUDE
IN ADVANCE

I'M SO GRATEFUL

I FORGIVE

I WANT
TO FEEL

NOTES & EPIPHANIES

VISIONS & GUIDES

OVERCOMING BELIEFS

Is there something you want reeeeeeally bad, but you don't see evidence of it in your life experience? Could it be that subconsciously (or maybe consciously), you have a core belief that is preventing that desire from manifesting? Maybe you don't believe it is possible or that you're worthy of receiving it?

This is known as resistance. If what animates life is energy, then *resistance* prevents that energy from flowing. No matter how truly, madly or deeply you want something, the energy to create it can never coalesce when opposition to the manifestation is present. Often this resistance arises as a result of self-doubt, fear or attachment. We think that we (or our situation) has to change before we can fulfill our deepest desires. Or maybe we are afraid of what will happen when the manifestation is real. When we bring light to the resistant thoughts preventing the manifestation, and appreciate that aspect of ourselves or life experience, we transmute the resistance into amplification without ever having to change.

instructions

1. Write down what you want on the rope and then the "but" that always follows in the struggling pony. When you write this statement, feel for an emotional reaction. Did your energetic center feel like it embraced or resisted this statement? Record your resistance level in the space provided.

2. Appreciate the aspect of yourself that is preventing this desire from manifesting and write it in the free pony. Maybe you don't think you deserve it because you're lazy or because you were born to the wrong parents or because you never had parents or because society is against you. Take a moment to deeply appreciate that aspect of your life experience. Again, feel for an embrace or rejection of this statement. Record your resistance level now.

FURTHER READING

THE BIG LEAP BY GAY HENDRICKS

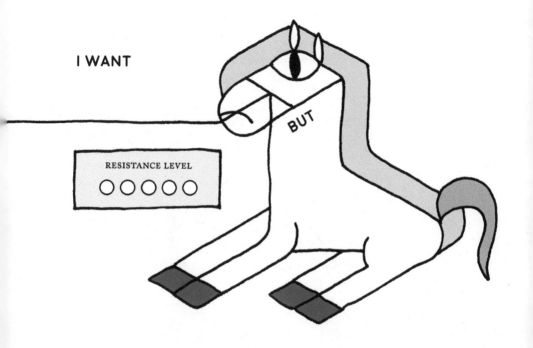

I WANT

BUT

RESISTANCE LEVEL
○○○○○

I APPRECIATE THE PART OF ME THAT

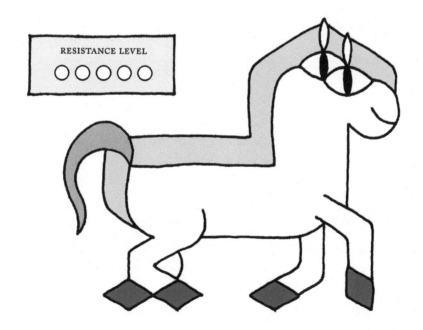

RESISTANCE LEVEL
○○○○○

DATE

DREAM

MOON PHASE
●◐◑◓○○○◑◐

Question

TIME

ANSWERS

ANSWERS

ANSWERS

CAST A
SPELL

I'M SWITCHING TO THE VERSION
OF REALITY I PREFER. IN THE
REALITY I PREFER...

PRE-PAVE

EVENT TITLE

BEFORE

DURING

AFTER

I INTEND

I PRAY

I LOVE

GRATITUDE
IN ADVANCE

I'M SO GRATEFUL

I FORGIVE

I WANT
TO FEEL

NOTES & EPIPHANIES

VISIONS & GUIDES

SPELL FOR

L⊙VE

Paramhansa Yogananda was an Indian guru and yogi responsible for introducing millions of Indians and Westerners to yoga and meditation in the first half of the 1900s. His most important lesson was to "love god."

But what does it mean to love god? According to many spiritual traditions, god is everything. All that we experience and beyond, including ourselves, is god. So to love god means to love it all. Every single little thing in your life. Every person, every annoying habit, every political outrage and crime against humanity. Love it all. And how do you love it? By distancing yourself from your thoughts and reuniting with Who You Really Are.

Learning to love it all is our greatest challenge here on earth. Our minds hate and resist and fear. It's hard to love the bad things people do, or the suffering we witness every day. But to lift the veil of illusion and attain peace of mind (therefore peace on earth), we must love.

instructions
Think of all the things you hate. All the things that annoy you. All the bad things that happen in your day. And then love them. They are god, and with love they will reveal their true perfection to you.

After each "I love you _____," insert the thing you hate. Then color in the halo of light around the thing you hate, and imagine sending peace and harmony to this thing. God is in everything, and when you practice loving all things, god will be revealed to you.

FURTHER READING

AUTOBIOGRAPHY OF A YOGI BY PARAMHANSA YOGANANDA

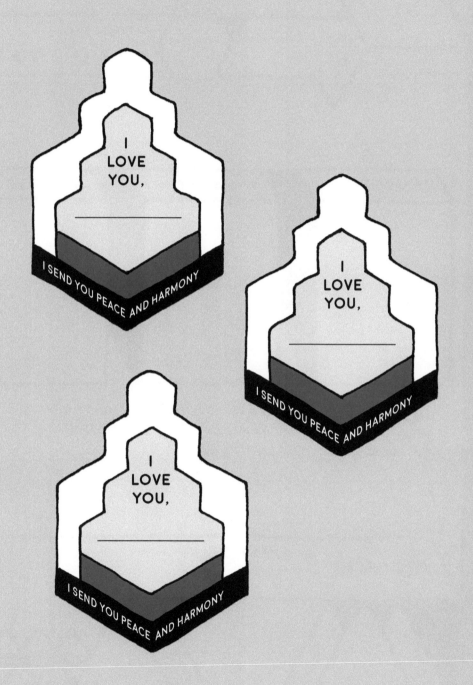

DATE

DREAM

MOON PHASE

QUESTION

TIME

ANSWERS

ANSWERS

ANSWERS

CAST A SPELL

I'M SWITCHING TO THE VERSION OF REALITY I PREFER. IN THE REALITY I PREFER...

PRE-PAVE

EVENT TITLE

BEFORE

DURING

AFTER

I INTEND

I PRAY

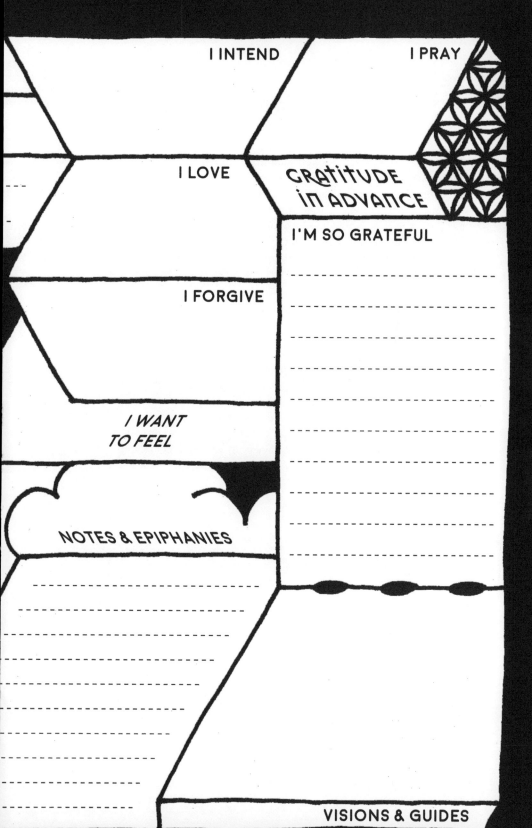

I LOVE

GRATITUDE IN ADVANCE

I'M SO GRATEFUL

I FORGIVE

I WANT
TO FEEL

NOTES & EPIPHANIES

VISIONS & GUIDES

SPELL FOR
FEELING BETTER

As Abraham-Hicks teaches, your emotions are your guidance system here on earth. They help you know if you are headed in the right direction. When you feel good, you are in alignment with source energy. When you feel bad, something is off. It's as simple as that. When you feel good, life reflects that good feeling and everything you want flows your way. When you feel bad, you push life away. When you feel bad, that is source energy's way of telling you you're off track. "Come back to me," source beckons. It's easy to feel good. When you feel good no matter what, nothing else matters.

instructions
Write a list of your go-to ways to feel good and then do a few of them. Record how you feel before and after. Color in the stars on the left to rate how you feel before the activity, and color the stars to the right of the blank after. Do you feel better now? Do you feel more optimistic about life? As your day goes on, pay attention to how you feel. The moment you start to feel bad, go back to your list and do it until you feel better. After feeling better, does your day start to click into place? Record the positive manifestations that come about as a result of feeling better.

POSITIVE MANIFESTATIONS

_____

_____

_____

_____

_____

_____

FURTHER READING

GETTING INTO THE VORTEX BY ESTHER AND JERRY HICKS

1.
2.
3.
4.
5.
6.
7.
8.
9.
10.

DATE ········ DREAM

MOON PHASE
●●◐◑◒○◓◔◕

QUESTION

TIME

- -

- -

ANSWERS   ANSWERS   ANSWERS

CAST A   I'M SWITCHING TO THE VERSION
SPELL   OF REALITY I PREFER. IN THE
                REALITY I PREFER...

- -

- -

PRE-PAVE ···· EVENT TITLE

BEFORE   DURING   AFTER

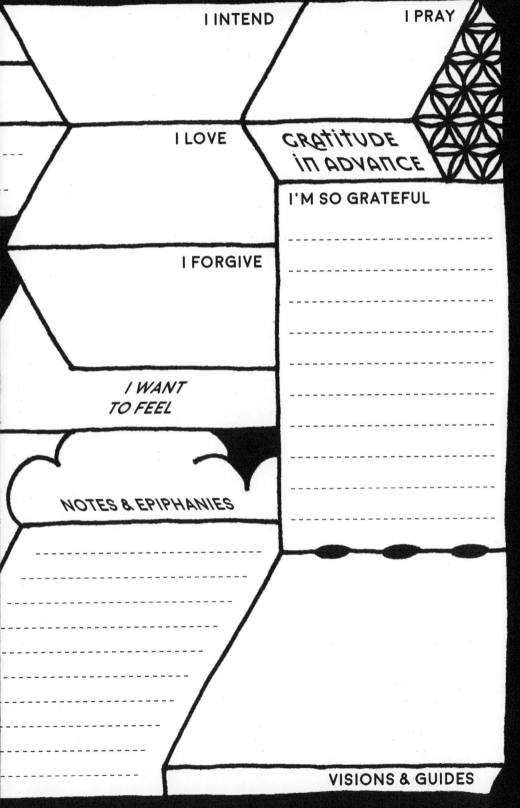

I INTEND

I PRAY

I LOVE

GRATITUDE
IN ADVANCE

I'M SO GRATEFUL

I FORGIVE

I WANT
TO FEEL

NOTES & EPIPHANIES

VISIONS & GUIDES

LiFE DESiGn

Technology is a tool, and it can be utilized in both positive and negative ways. This applies especially to our mobile devices, the ubiquitous, anxiety-producing miniature computers that we all love (and sometimes hate). What if we could skew the ratio more towards love and feel a little less addicted to scrolling?

The answer to falling in love with your technology (and yourself) is to be a creator instead of a consumer. It can be draining to wistfully look at everyone else's life and compare what's lacking in ours. But we can choose to set the bar instead of trying to meet it.

What's the goal of social sharing? For some the goal is accolades or validation, but what if you use the magnificent tools technology provides as a way of documenting all that is good (or that you want more of) in your reality?

The practice of documenting what you want more of puts you in a mode of looking for what you want to see. And when you look for reasons to celebrate life, you find them! This is magick in its truest form: you intend to create something, then you look for evidence of that creation and document it.

instructions
Use the space provided to create a storyboard for the movie of your life. What shots will you be looking to capture? What is the mood or message of your documentary? What's the moral of the story? As you move throughout your day, keep an eye out for all that you want to see in your life and document it. It doesn't have to be a movie. It can be photos, words or even your own illustration. Whatever it is you want, LOOK FOR IT, and then document when you see it.

FURtHER READinG

INEVITABLE BY KEVIN KELLY

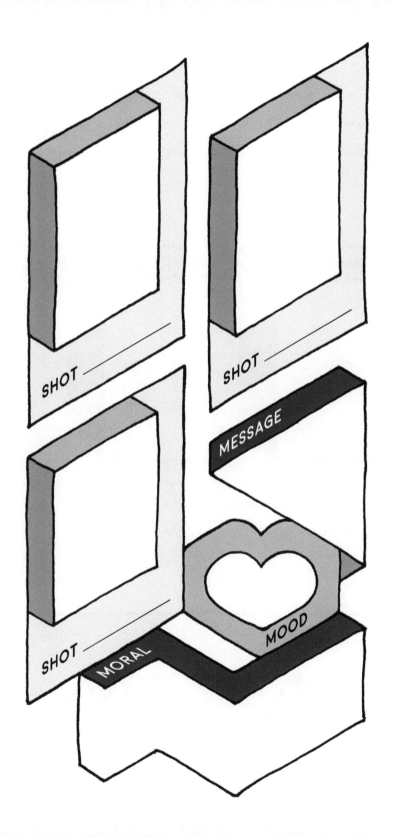

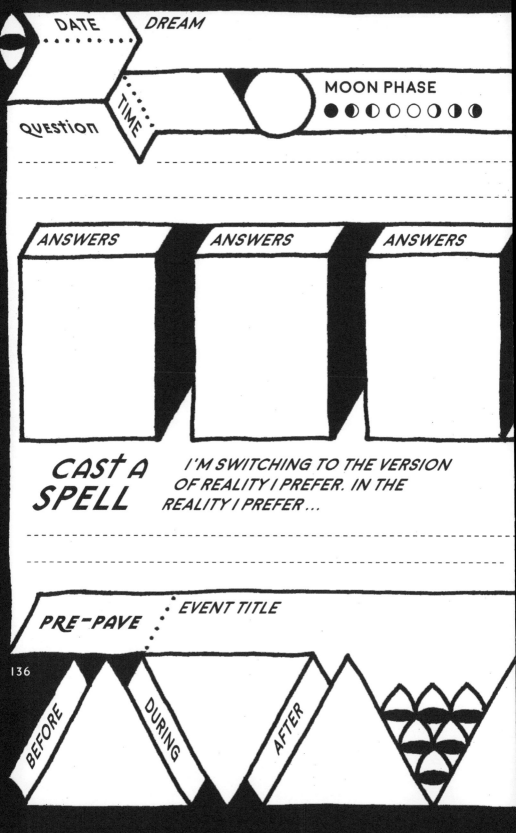

DATE

DREAM

QUESTION

TIME

MOON PHASE

ANSWERS

ANSWERS

ANSWERS

CAST A SPELL

I'M SWITCHING TO THE VERSION OF REALITY I PREFER. IN THE REALITY I PREFER ...

PRE-PAVE

EVENT TITLE

BEFORE

DURING

AFTER

I INTEND

I PRAY

I LOVE

GRATITUDE
IN ADVANCE

I'M SO GRATEFUL

I FORGIVE

I WANT
TO FEEL

NOTES & EPIPHANIES

VISIONS & GUIDES

SPELL FOR
connection

You think you have problems, but the only problem you ever have is disconnection. When you are disconnected from the infinite version of yourself, you feel something is missing. You might think it's money or a partner or possessions, but as soon as you obtain one of those, you will look for another outside source to fill the infinite hole within. It will never be enough.

You think if you solve your "problem," you will feel better. You think you will feel relieved, happy, fulfilled or safe. But have you ever noticed that getting what you want never fills you up? That new car smell wears off and you're still the same person. Or you hang out with your crush but the time you had isn't enough and you need more and more and more to fill the void.

There's no certainty in an ever-changing world, and if you allow something outside of you to be your reason for feeling good, you will feel bad when that situation changes. However, if your reason for feeling good is because you know that you are god in human form and that nothing can ever sever the tie you have with the magick of life, you will never have to feel bad no matter what happens (or doesn't happen). If that job falls through and you become destitute and have to live on the streets with your cat on a leash, you will still have access to the infinite love and satisfaction within.

instructions

1. What do I think will make me happy?

2. Why do I think it will make me happy?

3. Now ask your infinite self for advice or opinions on the matter. What do you hear?

FURTHER READING

DIE TO LIVE BY MAHARAJ CHARAN SINGH

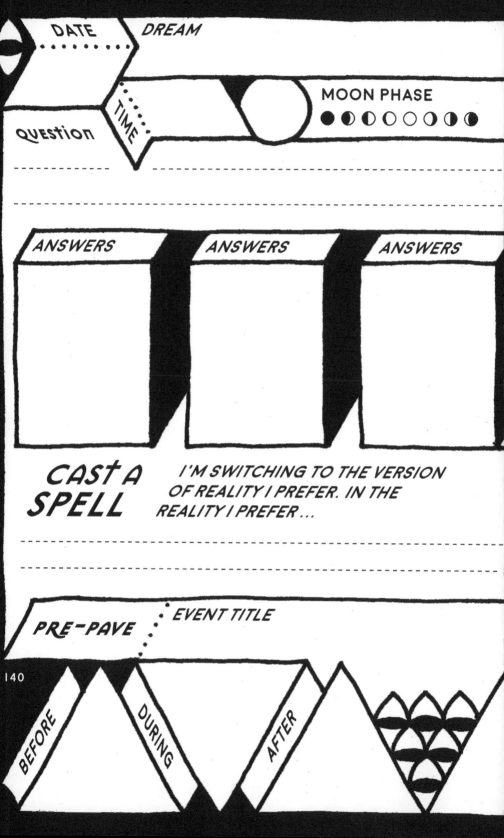

DATE

DREAM

QUESTION

TIME

MOON PHASE
●◐◐◑○○◑◐◑

ANSWERS

ANSWERS

ANSWERS

CAST A SPELL

I'M SWITCHING TO THE VERSION OF REALITY I PREFER. IN THE REALITY I PREFER...

PRE-PAVE

EVENT TITLE

BEFORE

DURING

AFTER

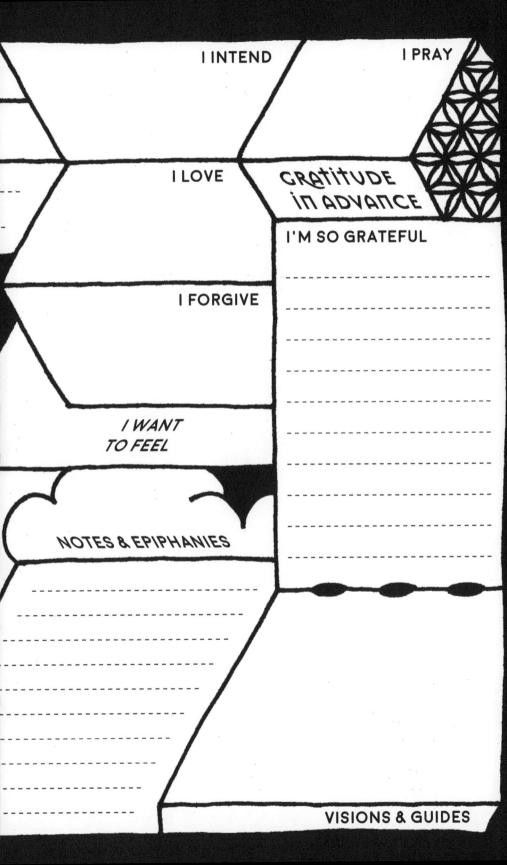

I INTEND

I PRAY

I LOVE

GRATITUDE
IN ADVANCE

I'M SO GRATEFUL

I FORGIVE

I WANT
TO FEEL

NOTES & EPIPHANIES

VISIONS & GUIDES

ENLIGHTENMENT

> "A lot of people try to counteract the 'I am not good enough' with 'I am good enough.' In other words, they take the opposite and they try to invest it. That still keeps the world at the level of polarities. The art is to go behind the polarities. So the act is to go not to the world of 'I am good' to counteract 'I am bad,' or 'I am lovable' as opposed to 'I am unlovable.' But go behind it to 'I am.' I am. I am. And 'I am' includes the fact that I do crappy things and I do beautiful things and I am. That includes everything and I am." RAM DASS

We live in the world of duality. We can't have rich without poor. We can't have knowing without ignorance. We can't have happiness without sadness. Your emotional highs are only as powerful as your lows. When you ride the rollercoaster of duality, you can get seasick from all the ups and downs.

We can transcend duality and return to the peace of oneness with the universe. You aren't good or bad; you just are. The circumstances in your life just are. They aren't good or bad. They exist. When you are able to observe yourself and your life experience without judgement clouding your perception, you feel at peace with everything that is.

instructions
Fill the frame with the words "I AM." Try breathing in as you write "I" and breathing out as you write "AM." Continue until you fill the page. Measure your light level before and after using the sun charts below.

BEFORE   AFTER

If your mind tries to put something after "I AM," don't let it. You're nothing and everything all at once and one word or phrase could never describe who or what you are. You are and that's enough.

FURTHER READING

BE HERE NOW BY RAM DASS

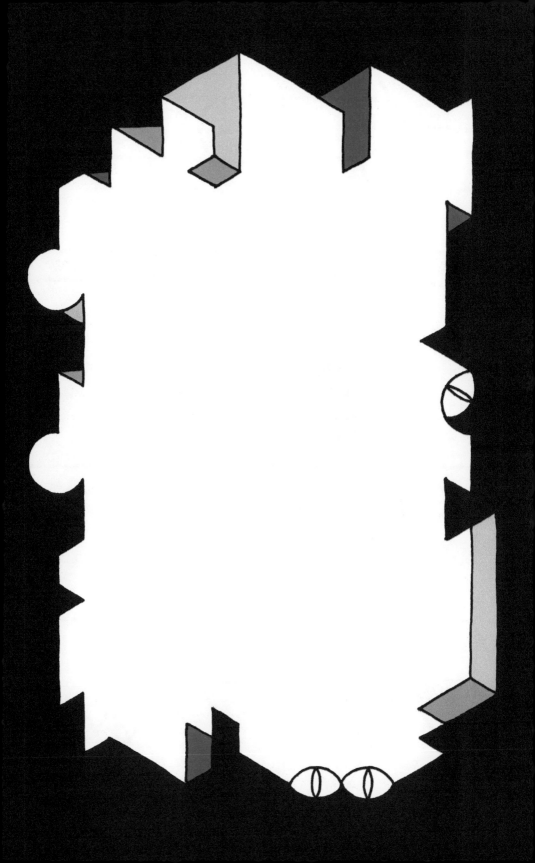

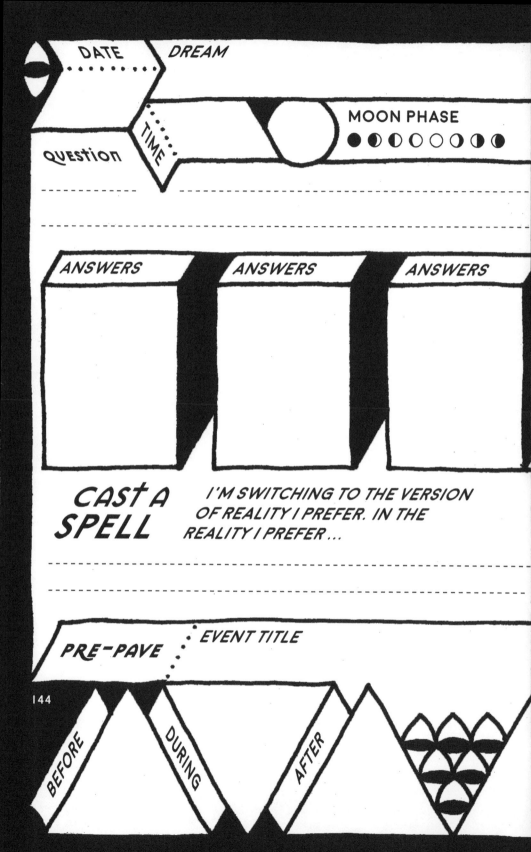

DATE DREAM

QUESTION TIME

MOON PHASE

ANSWERS ANSWERS ANSWERS

CAST A SPELL

I'M SWITCHING TO THE VERSION OF REALITY I PREFER. IN THE REALITY I PREFER...

PRE-PAVE EVENT TITLE

BEFORE DURING AFTER

I INTEND

I PRAY

I LOVE

GRATITUDE
IN ADVANCE

I'M SO GRATEFUL

- - - - - - - - - - - - - - - - - -

- - - - - - - - - - - - - - - - - -

- - - - - - - - - - - - - - - - - -

I FORGIVE

- - - - - - - - - - - - - - - - - -

- - - - - - - - - - - - - - - - - -

- - - - - - - - - - - - - - - - - -

I WANT
TO FEEL

- - - - - - - - - - - - - - - - - -

- - - - - - - - - - - - - - - - - -

- - - - - - - - - - - - - - - - - -

NOTES & EPIPHANIES

- - - - - - - - - - - - - - - - - -

- -

- -

- -

- -

- -

- -

- -

- -

VISIONS & GUIDES

SPELL FOR
LASTING SUCCESS

Now that you've worked through 30 exercises in this book, you've probably enjoyed some more than others. Some were probably very effective while others not at all. Every person is different and each technique, process and mantra speaks differently to all.

What you've also probably caught onto is that which process you choose is not nearly as important as your devotion to the process. When you really do the work, you see the results. When you don't resonate with a particular process, it can be difficult to see or feel results.

instructions
Reflect on the past month and take note of your favorite and most effective processes. Which one was the hardest? What category do you lean towards? What do you want to work on? Use this knowledge to create your own techniques based on what works for you.

FURTHER READING

THE BOOK OF SECRETS BY OSHO

CATEGORIES

GRATITUDE
MANTRAS
CHANNELING
CONSCIOUSNESS
INTENTION
TRANSMUTATION
VISUALIZATION

EFFECTIVE

WORK ON

FAVORITE

HARDEST